From Hero To Zero

by Charles L. ("Chuck") Panici

Table of Contents

Preface
The Purpose Of This Book

First I want to thank you for buying, or borrowing or otherwise taking the time to read my book. It's the first and only book I've ever written. I've always been better at doing things than writing about them. I've had the help of journalist who is almost as old and wise to the ways of the world as me, even though he's a Canadian who has a habit of putting a "u" in "color" and "neighbor." But we got rid of those.

I'm telling you my story for two reasons. One is very personal; the other is social. On one hand I write about particular people and particular events. On the other I'm talking about issues that affect each and every citizen of the United States of America.

You may be aware that I served four consecutive terms as mayor of Chicago Heights, from 1975 to 1991. When I took office the city was an ethnically divided industrial tank town with a decaying infrastructure and an antiquated water supply that had to be chemically treated just to make it drinkable. By the time I left office Chicago Heights was a town people are proud to live in. We have a state-of-the-art water system bringing fresh drinking water inland from Lake Michigan, up-to-date public services and a well functioning infrastructure on an organized maintenance schedule.

You may also be aware that during that same era I developed a number of strategies of political organization, strategies and systems that are as effective in a local election campaign as they are in a state or national vote. I was able to advance the cause of the Republican Party throughout my own city and our Bloom Township area. I became Republican committeeman for Bloom Township. My organization was a big influence in the election of governors, senators, congressmen, judges and plenty of other public officials.

If you know all this you probably also know that in

1993 I and my two dear friends and colleagues, John Gliottoni and Louise Marshall, were indicted, tried and convicted on criminal charges of extorting bribes and kickback payments from contractors and businesses that had dealings with the city. I served eight years of a ten year sentence and was ordered to pay well over a million dollars in fines and "restitution." The quotation marks around "restitution" signify that those criminal charges were trumped up, the trial rigged and the imprisonment of the three defendants was a travesty.

Why? Because crimes really were committed. There really had been bribes and kickbacks. But all the evidence pointed to the guilt of four felons who testified for the prosecution. It was obvious that those four were the real criminals, yet it was they who went free while three innocent people were convicted. What those four did was wrong; they committed the *mortal sin of bearing false witness* against innocent people. But morally and ethically, *the federal prosecutors were even worse!* From the very beginning their plan was to bribe and coerce witnesses, distort the facts, conceal evidence, trample the truth and just plain lie their way to victory.

How could such an injustice be allowed to happen in a country that promises "justice for all" in its Pledge of Allegiance? Why do prosecutors, especially the feds, work so hard at convicting the innocent? In my case there's the possibility of a political motive, and that's a trail that has the potential of winding its way to some smoke filled back room, maybe as far away as Pennsylvania Avenue.

That's what my book is about. And I'm not the only one who has been steamrollered by a vindictive and arbitrary justice department. Since 1970 there have been at least 2,500 cases similar to mine. People imprisoned for crimes they didn't commit!

A question that lawyers often ask in the course of a trial is, "Who stood to profit from this?" As you hear my side of the story, and look at the facts I'm going to show you, keep that question in mind. You will see clearly that the careers of several participants in the affair did very well afterwards. The publicity and prestige were a valuable prize for them. But were there others, behind the scenes and even far away from Chicago, who wanted a successful and prominent Republican like Chuck Panici out of the way?

These aren't questions that we can settle in a single book. That's why there's a website – www.chuckpanici.com – and a Facebook page where more information is available and issues can be discussed (or debated) in a fair and open forum.

Foreword
Where I'm Coming From

"Here's the deal, Mr. Panici. You tell us who killed the Spilotro brothers and we can make all of this go away."

That's a US attorney, talking to the me, former Mayor of Chicago Heights, Illinois. He's offering me a deal. If I'm willing to tell a few whopping lies, he's willing to drop a long list of trumped up criminal charges. And he can really do it. He really has that kind of power. That's the way the Department of Justice can build a case. That's why they win ninety per cent of the time. They know how to stack the deck.

And these are serious charges. They include five RICO counts, brought under the Racketeer Influenced and Corrupt Organizations Act. Charges that can put you away for a long, long time if you're found guilty.

In truth, the prosecutor didn't speak directly to me. His message came through my lawyer after I learned I was about to be indicted. You know what it is to be indicted? It's horrible! Everything lands on you all at once. A shock runs through your whole body. I said, "John, you have to be kidding, right?" Sadly enough he wasn't.

So how did this nightmare begin, this nightmare that was to haunt me and my family for the next twenty years? I knew I was in for the fight of my life but I had no idea how many rounds it was going to go. I still don't know. We still aren't finished.

And why am I writing my story years after being released from prison, where I served a little over eight years of a ten year sentence for crimes I didn't commit? Because the whole thing is wrong. Because the process of crime and punishment has been so twisted out of shape that our Justice Department too often becomes an enemy of justice. Stick with me through this story and I'll prove it. I'll show you how.

I intend to show you how government lawyers, working with the FBI, manufactured a criminal case and pinned it on three honest municipal officials, three commissioners of the City of Chicago Heights. Not just honest commissioners but recognized achievers of excellence. Three commissioners who had made history by creating a modern water system, bringing fresh water to their community, expanding the city's tax base by bringing the Ford Motor Company into their city as a taxpayer. A city administration whose efforts were recognized by two presidents of the United States, four Illinois governors, US senators, a congressman and dozens of famous people in business, sports and entertainment.

These prosecutors tore all that down for their own personal gain, to advance their own careers. They cooked up outrageous lies to justify their case. They defamed a respected, God fearing, 72 year old black woman, by alleging she shook down a high ranking Mob boss. Can you beat that one? The script writers at the US Justice Department borrowed a lot from TV as they cobbled together their piece of legal theater. But the mass media didn't care about authenticity; they gobbled it up. Anything to do with the Mob is always good for headlines.

Only one problem - no evidence.

Next I'll show you how the feds actually did nail a real crook, a man named Nick LoBue, who had lied his entire adult life, stolen money from his own father and extorted kickback payments from city contractors. You will see how, instead of prosecuting this crook like they should have done, they let offered to him walk on the condition that he would get on the witness stand and denounce three honest people. There's a word for that. They call it "plea bargaining," a polite way to say "bribery," a tactic that all too often convicts innocent people and allows liars and thieves to walk.

They pulled the same trick with other felons they wanted to use as witnesses. Promised them leniency, even total immunity from prosecution. All these people had to do was get up and lie on the witness stand, follow the script the prosecutors wrote for them. And why? To make the government lawyers and the FBI agents look like winners, further their careers, get them promotions. Did their scheme actually serve the cause of justice? You tell me! Three honest, hard working people went to prison while the guy who committed all the crimes, the guy who stole from the taxpayers to pay his gambling debts, got a slap on the wrist and went free.

One of these prosecutors, a guy named Fred Foreman, had ambitions to become governor of Illinois. He didn't quite get that far but he did get to be a judge. Not bad! Another prosecutor, Chris Gair, later left the government service to become a defense attorney with a high priced Chicago law firm. He defends – get this! – people charged with white collar crimes, including politicians.

Gair is still as slick as he was in the early 90s, but now his job is to get people off instead of sending them up the river. And he makes a lot more money than the government was ever willing to pay him.

I'll show you another thing. There's a reason why these lawyers were able to hoodwink a jury with their faked evidence and dishonest arguments. The judge who conducted the trial admitted weak and even fabricated evidence against us but excluded other evidence that might have exonerated us. That judge was James B. Zagel, who had been on the bench only two years, a former prosecutor – never a defense attorney - and director of the Illinois state police, a writer of crime fiction who at one point quoted P.T. Barnum in the courtroom. In fairness to him, he may well have been threatened with prosecution himself if he had failed to support the prosecutors' case. It wouldn't be the first time that's been done!

Whatever the reasons for his attitude, Judge Zagel had no business hearing a case involving me. He was appointed to the bench by President Ronald Reagan. President Reagan appointed Zagel on the recommendation of the Republican governor of Illinois, Jim Thompson. Governor Thompson recommended Zagel on the advice of his Republican Party officials. One of those officials was me, Charles Panici, Republican Party Committeeman for Bloom Township. Oh, the irony!

People might say Judge Zagel owed a quite a debt of gratitude to Chuck Panici. If he was aware of that debt, he might have felt he had to be extra tough to avoid any appearance that he might be taking it easy on a defendant who had helped advance his career. The fact is that he shouldn't have heard the case at all. Maybe my legal team should have entered a motion to recuse Judge Zagel. But the truth is that he should have "recused" (removed) himself.

I'll show you plenty of other things too. I'll tell you the highlights of my life story, how I came to be mayor of Chicago Heights, Illinois. How I became a leading political organizer for the Republican Party, where I'm still to this day a go-to guy for people who want to run for public office. I'll tell you how I was approached by Ronald Reagan while he was still the governor of California and when he came to speak at Bloom Township High School after he was elected to be president of the United States. How I met and welcomed Vice-President and later President George H. W. Bush five times to Chicago Heights. And how I came to know so many other famous figures in politics, business, sports and the entertainment industry.

And when I've shown you everything, when you've looked past the smoke and mirrors and seen all the facts, I think you'll reach your own verdict on Chuck Panici. At the very least I think you'll find me "presumptively innocent" - in other words, not proven guilty beyond a reasonable doubt. Or at best I think you may find me both legally and literally innocent. You may conclude that none of us, Louise Marshall, John Gliottoni or myself, should ever have been indicted, much less tried and certainly not convicted. I'm not looking for an appeal or even a new trial. Experience has shown me that we simply can't trust the system. Instead I look to you, the reader, for an honest verdict.

You be the judge on this one.

I can tell you one thing before we even start. I don't know who killed the Spilotro brothers. I don't know who killed John F. Kennedy either, and I don't know where Jimmy Hoffa is buried. So what happened? One minute I'm shaking hands with the president of the United States; the next I'm being asked, "Who killed the Spilotro brothers?"

You may remember the Spilotro brothers. They were the two organized crime guys, fictionalized in the movie Casino, who were buried (some say alive!) in an Indiana corn field. Well much to my dismay the FBI decided in its wisdom that Chuck Panici might know something about that. They should have asked Robert de Niro, Joe

Pesci or Don Rickles. Those guys knew a lot more than me because they were in the movie and read the script.

One of the guys suspected of masterminding the Spilotro murders was Albert "Caesar" Tocco, an Italian-American who grew up a block and a half from my home in Chicago Heights. He was a couple of years older than me, and he grew up to be an important "wise guy" in the Chicago Outfit. Tocco was never convicted of anyone's murder, but in 1988 the Feds did succeed in putting him away for a total of 200 years.

My name is Charles "Chuck" Panici. I'm an American who happens to be of Italian descent. I'm not Tony "The Big Tuna" Accardo, John "The Dapper Don" Gotti or Joey "The Clown" Lombardo. Maybe the FBI came after me because I grew up in the south suburbs of Chicago in a neighborhood called Hungry Hill. Maybe because I hung around with guys with names like Sam "Hobo" Cianchetti, Giulio "Mcollough" Perozzi, and Dominic "Mimi" Falaschetti. Was I a suspect for being Italian? For hanging with the wrong crowd?

They have some very tough gangsters in London, England too - racketeers, killers and drug barons with names like Tim Smith and Dick McLean. Recently I heard of a guy they call "Johnnie Two Times" because he says everything twice. Does it follow that all the Smiths and McLeans have got to be gangsters just because they have a certain name? Go figure.

I've never had so much as a speeding ticket. I pay my taxes and I support my family. And by the way, you want to know about Sam "Hobo" Cianchetti? Well, he is a retired California Superior Court judge. In fact he and I still have dinner together whenever he's in town. Giulio "Mcollough" Perozzi - God rest his soul! - ran a successful business for over fifty years before he passed away last year. And Dominic "Mimi" Falaschetti? He was an art teacher; we were really proud of him because he was the first one of us that went to college. No murderers here, just hard working, successful Italian Americans like myself who were able to beat the odds.

Back in the twenties, thirties and forties there were neighborhoods like ours all over America. You had no more control over who grew up next door to you or who you saw on the playground than you do today. Compare the Hill to the inner city neighborhoods of today. The social problems that existed then are still with us. Inner city kids don't have a lot of choices. They can go to honest work at a fast food restaurant for minimum wage, work forty hours a week and pay taxes. Or they can go the easier but riskier route pushing something illegal, work a street corner for cash a couple of hours a day. It's the same choice of lifestyle today as it was in the old days.

Sure, there were guys who grew up on the hill who might have been a little unscrupulous. But this is America, we are told, home to all sorts of people, good and bad. Being in the Outfit, having "Cosa Nostra" associated with your name is the same kind of stereotype as being Black and being associated with the "Gangster Disciples." That is no more fair to the kid who works at McDonalds, than it is to guys like Hobo or Mimi or myself who worked our asses off so we could beat the odds and make better choices. We were all under the same pressures as kids today, dreaming bigger dreams of success in life.

20

Chapter One
The Good Old Days On Hungry Hill

Hungry Hill in Chicago Heights, Illinois is a neighborhood about thirty miles south of the famous Chicago Loop. Chicago Heights was called "The City of Industry" and is still known as "The Crossroads of the Nation." Truth to tell, the Hill isn't much of a hill. Somebody from Colorado or Wyoming would say it's flat as a pancake.

I was raised at 22nd and Wallace, across the street from Petrarca Park. I was the middle child, the third of five. The front of our house was the family store and bar, *3 Star Liquor*. Hell, I remember tending bar when I was fourteen years old. In those days it was not unusual to help out with the family business, with no age restrictions. It was just like the harvest season in the country when kids would take time off school to help their families on the farm. It really was a different time back then.

I think my parents must have been the two hardest
working people I have ever known. My father was
Cesare Panici. He was about as far from a "wise guy"
mobster as you can get. It would have made Cesare
Panici shudder to hear his name mentioned in the same
sentence as a word like Mafia, Camorra or Cosa Nostra.

He and my mother, Josephine Cimaroli, arrived at
different times in the United States through Ellis Island
in the early 1900s. They were both from the small town
of Amaseno in the Central Italian province of Frosinone

in the region of Lazio, just south of Rome. They were typical hard working Italian country people with nothing but good values, a strong work ethic and the all American dream of a better life.

People tell me that Lazio is the very region that two thousand years ago was called Latium, "Home of the Latins," where the ancient Romans and the Latin language came from. The old Romans had some things in common with the modern Panici's. They valued the family, worked hard, respected honor and virtue, helped each other get ahead. That was how they built a nation and a civilization that has lasted thousands of years.

In the 1980s I visited Italy with my father. I remember him speaking to the local people, telling them how proud he was of his family in America. My mother didn't even want to go back to Italy. She would say, "What do I want to go back there for? I have everything I need right here."

My parents' attitude rubbed off on me. The values I was raised with are the values I still live by today and have always lived by. To work hard, to treat people the way I expect to be treated, to help as many people as possible on the way - those are values that I learned from my mother and father. They didn't just survive the Great Depression; they never even complained about it.

 I grew up in the house where my mother's family had lived when they first came to America. My father eventually bought the place and until a few years ago it was still in the family. My father, as I said, was a hard working man. He worked for the City of Chicago Heights water department until he retired. But he wanted more. After all he was raising a family of seven. So in the late forties he called a family meeting and we talked about what kind of business the family could get into. We considered going into the pizza business because it was something pretty new to America. We also talked about going into the bar business with carry outs and delivery.

My brothers Phil, Kelo and myself helped my father decide that we would go into the bar business and that's what we did. That was the beginning of *3 Star Liquor*. The store still sits at 22nd and Wallace in Chicago Heights and the original sign still hangs from its rooftop. The bocce courts are still out in the back yard and some of America's best bocce players still gather there on Wednesdays. In all honesty I have to admit that I'm one of them.

I still see on a very regular basis the guys that I grew up with, at least the ones that have not yet passed away. These are friendships that have more than survived the passing of time. We go back 75 years, but it feels like yesterday when we formed our gang. Our gang was not the kind of gang that the government accused me of associating with. We were the CHEBS (The "Chicago Heights Eagle Beak Society"), not a vicious organized crime syndicate. And we were not very organized. The only requirement for membership was that you had to have a big "Roman eagle beak" Italian nose, something that was not lacking in our neighborhood. The president of the club was T.I. "Tony" Iacobucci because T.I. always had the biggest nose. The joke was that if we had just one of our noses filled with quarters we would be rich.

Again, that was our group. But just over on the next block there were guys growing up and going in a very different direction. Guido Fidanzi, for example, ended up getting shot coming out of the bathroom of Malizia's gas station on the East Side one afternoon in broad daylight. Albert Tocco, who lived on that next block over, ended up being a top man in the Chicago Outfit. He was eventually sentenced to 200 years and died in prison.

That was the neighborhood I grew up in.

One of the toughest times for my family was when we lost my brother Joe during World War Two. He was one of the many Chicago Heights Italian Americans who gave their lives fighting for freedom and for the America we loved. My brothers and sister were very close. My brother Joe died in the war and my brother Phil passed away about a week before I was indicted. So it happened that in March of 1992 I lost my wife, my older brother and eventually my freedom.

I guess a lot of people might have crumbled in the face of that many misfortunes one after another. I did not, and I'll tell you why. I have attitude on my side. I don't mean the "attitude" that rap artists talk about. My kind of attitude takes learning, training and practice. And once you've got it, nobody can ever take it away from you. I got my attitudinal learning from some of the best teachers in history. The first was Napoleon Hill, the Big Daddy of attitudinal training. Later came Charles Swindoll, founder of Insight For Living and author of one of my favorite sayings.

"I am convinced that life is 10% what happens to me and 90% how I react to it. And so it is with you . . .we are in charge of our attitudes."

The other thing that makes me strong is my family. When I went away to prison my cousin Fiore Benedetti's wife Rose made a *novena* (a promise to God) that she would cook a meal for me once a week when I got back, a promise she has kept since 2001 when I got back home. So you know where to find me every Friday at twelve noon sharp. Don't be late and you better be hungry.

My brother Kelo and sister Phyllis took over and ran the family business, *3 Star Liquors*, where Governor Big Jim Thompson would later announce his run for Governor of Illinois in 1978. That *3 Star* building is where we all grew up. My father built the famous bocce courts there. My brother Phil ran his very successful sign business out of the old garage. I had offices for my advertising business, *Happily Ever After,* upstairs. *3 Star* was not just a package liquor store; it was a place where family worked and played together for three generations. All of the kids, my brothers and my family worked there through the years, and my greatest memories are of that place.

I married the love of my life, Dolores Jean Falcioni, in 1950. We were married for 42 years before she passed away in 1992, about two weeks before I was indicted. We met at Bloom High School and it was love at first sight. I was the captain of the basketball team and she was a cheer leader. She lit up a room when she walked in, then and right up till the time of her passing. Dolores was from the East side of Chicago Heights and, me being from The Hill, they said it would never work out because in those days you weren't supposed to marry outside of your neighborhood. But it did work out. We went on to raise four kids together. And if it weren't for my four kids, I tell you again, I would never have survived the living hell of my trial and imprisonment. Debbie, Chuckie Junior, Joey and Tami, and their families, are the reason I am fighting to tell my story and clear my name.

I don't want my grandchildren and great grandchildren to think Papa was a bad guy. I want them to know the truth, what really happened, the things I accomplished for my city, my party, my family and my friends. And as I promised at the beginning, I especially want to prove to you that I am not only an innocent man but the victim of a dirty trick. This was a plot that had nothing to do with justice and much to do with the personal ambitions of certain lawyers and policemen.

I owe much of my political success to my wife Dolores. She was always right behind me one hundred per cent of the time, encouraging me to go forward. She never complained about the long hours my business and political career took away from the family. She pretty much raised our kids while I worked at trying to make a better life for all of us. Perhaps the one good thing about her passing away in 1992 is that she didn't have to see her family go through the pain and suffering that lay ahead. I wonder what she would have thought when all the criminal accusations began. She was pretty feisty.

No one knows better than me that I'm not perfect. I wasn't a perfect mayor; I had my own business to manage at the same time I served as part time mayor, but I did my best for my city. I'm not fervently religious like my wife. I wasn't a perfect husband and father. People call me a workaholic; I let my wife carry more of the burden of raising our children than I did. But please know that I have always loved my wife and family, then and now, more than life itself.

I guess you've seen by now that my family means everything to me. I still have dinner at least two times a week with my sister Phyllis and her husband Don, and it

30

is not unusual for one of the kids or grand kids to show up depending on what aunty is cooking, so there is always family around. We're not very different from those ancient Roman ancestors.

And like me, those guys in the white togas had attitude.

Chapter Two
Chuck For Mayor

I've told you about my happy memories of the *3 Star*, which is still doing business at 22nd Street and Wallace in Chicago Heights, where I grew up with my parents, brothers and sister. But the *3 Star* was more than a home to our family. It was more than just a livelihood, although it provided good income for many, many years.

3 Star Liquor was also what municipal economists call an *anchor* - a business whose success drives everything around it. A good example of an anchor enterprise is a professional ballpark like Wrigley Field, home of the Chicago Cubs. The neighborhood surrounding Wrigley field is filled with bars and taverns serving baseball fans as they come and go. On the Hill the anchor was *3 Star Liquor*.

It was a social gathering place for the whole neighborhood. When the neighborhood was thriving the *3 Star* did well. When the neighborhood went through hard times so did the *3 Star*. And one of the big drawing cards was the *bocce* courts behind the store. They were my dad's idea. At that time there were not many *bocce*

32

courts around. Nowadays the game is widely played, but those *3 Star* courts have attracted serious players right down to this day.

Bocce was not well known in the early years of 20th century America but it has become very popular in recent times. Scholars tell us that *bocce* was first played by the ancient Egyptians - under a different name - and that the game traveled from Egypt to ancient Greece and then from Greece to Rome. It took a few thousand years for the game to spread, but now it's played in cities and towns throughout the United States and Canada. I've seen pictures of modern playing courts that look like the Chicago Stadium of bocce. I've even heard, although I can't confirm it, that my old friend and boyhood neighbor Jerry Colangelo is planning to add *bocce* courts to a number of hotels that he and his group have acquired.

I grew up on the Hill at a time when Chicago Heights was booming. At the time when the Second World War began Chicago Heights was listed in the Guinness book of records because it had the largest number of factories per city resident! The city was unique in other ways. A railway line running right through the middle of town separated the east side from the west side. That's why people used to say my dear wife Dolores and I were from "the wrong side of the tracks" for each other. Geographically they had a point. But romantically, how wrong they were!

The Hill was a working class neighborhood, but as I said before, we all had dreams of a better life. The block where we lived on 22nd street had ten homes. Three doors away from me lived Jerry Colangelo, who was to become one of America's most successful businessmen. I guess Jerry must now own most of Phoenix, Arizona. He sure has owned most of the sports teams at different times. Most recently Jerry has been running USA Basketball, picking the players who represent the United States in international competition. Since he took over, USA Basketball has not lost a single game, up to and including the 2012 Olympics in London.

Another neighbor on 22nd street was my dear old friend, Sam "Hobo" Cianchetti, the California Superior Court judge I spoke of earlier in this story. As I mentioned before, he and I still have dinner together whenever he's in town. And then of course there was me, Chuck Panici, four times elected mayor of Chicago Heights with majorities as high as 75%, builder and leader of one of the most influential political organizations in the United States, the Bloom Township Republican Party.

Not bad for ten houses in one block of a working class neighborhood in Chicago Heights!

How did I go from junior bartender to mayor and Republican committeeman? It took time and a lot of hard work. It all started for me, I think, when I got married. I found out I wasn't very smart and I had to do something better than working in a gas station. I was working three jobs which altogether paid me a total of maybe a hundred bucks a week.

Then I started studying attitudinal materials, self-help literature, and I taught myself. I have been doing self-help disciplines every day throughout my life. I learned a lot. I had no formal education, but I had that kind of self-administered education. I read books like *Think And Grow Rich* and *You Are What You Think You Are*. I trained myself to think I was a pretty good guy, whether it was true or not. I became a coordinator of the attitudinal program, *Adventures In Attitudes*. It's a very popular program. Tens of thousands of people have taken it.

I didn't develop the program; I coordinated it. It was a twenty-five hour program. I had hundreds of people go through it. A real good friend of mine, Bob Picha, probably put more than ten thousand people through the program himself. Bob and I became pretty good friends. We talked about it all the time. I learned how to brainstorm.

The result is that I believe attitude is everything. It starts with attitude and my approach is always to develop a relationship that produces a win-win situation. It takes a lot to accomplish and it's tough. And I think that view helped me in my political life. It helped me in my business life too, because I had a very successful business before all the troubles began. It goes to my father too. He helped me a lot. He was a great dad.

So there I was in 1950, just married and working three jobs for a hundred bucks a week. I needed to do something! So I went to work in a personnel office, Hotpoint, or General Electric at that time. Of course I had no education so they just put me to work, probably at minimum wage. So I found a second job in a tuxedo rental shop. In a way it was the job that found me.

I loved to play basketball in those days and the person that owned the tuxedo shop was also a basketball fan. We got ourselves into several leagues and I started to recruit some good basketball players, so we ended up doing really well as a team. The guy that owned the shop loved it. It wasn't making him any money but he loved the competition. And of course I eventually had to tell him I was going to have to quit playing basketball because I had to make a living.

At that point he said, "Why don't you come to work for me?" A good idea! And so it worked out that I was able to play basketball, work in the tuxedo shop and learn the business. Four or five years later it occurred to me that maybe I could do this kind of thing myself. So I went into the formal clothing rentals business on my own with a few dollars my dad gave me to get started.

My tuxedo rental business did quite well. So next I developed a new business inspired by the rental business. It was a bridal book called *Happily Ever After*, a trade publication for people in the bridal business: tuxedo rentals, gowns, catering, cakes, flowers and so on. There were twenty-three different kinds of people represented in the book. With our way of marketing it we opened up about twenty or thirty states.

About when all this was going on, in 1975, I decided to run for mayor and we sold the business as a going concern at a good honest value. And then I went into municipal politics. I really got started in politics before I was ever elected to office. I was a member of the Chicago Heights Chamber of Commerce and was given the job of organizing an effort to get a referendum

passed for some really necessary school funding.

Referendums were about as popular then as they are now, about as welcome as a broken shoe lace or a wad of gum stuck to the bottom of your shoe. It was a $10 million funding initiative. In today's economy with our shrunken dollar it would be $75 million. Remember, this was in 1963. So I put together a team with a guy named Fritz Nehnevay as my co-chair. I knew Fritz from playing basketball. He had business in the heights and we had become friends over the years.

People don't like taxes of course and I don't either, but we developed a little system to get out the vote, get people together and pretty much change people's attitude toward the situation. Because at that particular time and even now nobody likes to pay taxes. Nevertheless we passed our ten million dollar referendum. And that's how I got started. That was when the light bulb lit up. The organizational methods I used to get that referendum passed were the methods I've used throughout my political career.

There were a lot of people who liked what we were doing. And during our first campaign it happened that we were at a function where the mayor at the time was also present. And we were talking about the referendum. I had done a little research. And although I don't want to knock the guy, he didn't vote for or against. He didn't vote at all! He didn't take the time.

So I asked him, "How did you do at the referendum?"

"Oh I voted in favor of the referendum."

"No kidding! How about if I tell you didn't vote on the referendum?"

That really killed him with all the people who were at that meeting, people who were really interested in the referendum.

A big, big factor in the success of my campaign was my firm belief in the win-win. A lot of the people that I went to for help had never seen an organization process a plan. I showed them a plan and there was one guy, an old time Republican named Fred LoBue. No relation to the Nick LoBue we're going to meet later in this story! Fred was a township commissioner. And I made a presentation to see what kind of help I could get and, believe me, he helped quite a bit! He was the first guy to put up his hand and say, "I'm putting five hundred dollars on this guy!"

That was our first campaign donation. From there we raised enough money to do the campaign, but we still ended up with about a nine thousand dollar deficit. If we had lost I would have been committed to pay the nine thousand! But it never happened. We always had enough money from then on to do all the things we wanted to do. That's par for the game. That's how we started.

But somewhere along the line I still had to make a living because the office of mayor was only a part time job. I think it worked out to about eighteen cents an hour. So I came across an idea. We developed a program that collected money for hospitals. We called it a pre-collect. It wasn't a collection agency but it was very successful.

The program succeeded by collecting small balances that the hospitals just didn't have time to work. In the usual course of events, a thousand or two thousand dollar account balance to a hospital is no big deal. They don't even work them. But we found an inexpensive way to collect those small balances and it worked. It got into a win-win. It was good for us and it was good for them, and I just loved it. And that's what I've always tried to do. I always try to get into something where you create a relationship that's going to last for more than two weeks. I have a lifetime relationship with many people in that business.

Looking back at those times, you have to wonder that the government would thirty years later accuse a guy like me of extorting bribes! If someone in my position had been interested in conspiring to milk the public purse, wouldn't it have started right then in 1975, as soon as I got comfortable in public office? And yet all of the charges against me in 1991 related to crimes dating from the 1980s. I guess somehow I was supposed to have taught myself to be an extortionist without any previous experience! Does history tell of any self-taught racketeers?

As you will see, there certainly did exist a conspiracy to abuse the authority of public office but I was not a perpetrator; I was one of its victims. Then there were those "legal" conspirators, the lawyers of the Justice Department and the crooks they recruited to advance their game plan. But that comes later.

Chapter Three
How To Succeed As An Honest Politician

A lot of people say "honest politician" is an oxymoron, a self-contradicting expression.

It's not hard to see why. Again and again we hear of cases where public officials are caught with their hands in the till. But the fact is, the great majority of elected officials are honest. The fact that a few are without scruples is the reason the occasional scandal becomes big news.

I ran four times for the mayor's chair in Chicago Heights. I won every time. In one of those elections they said the voters gave me a 75% majority. During my four terms in office I was able to do a lot for my city. Together with my fellow commissioners, I organized one of the most important infrastructure projects any American city has seen. We brought fresh drinking water from Lake Michigan inland through a pipeline to Chicago Heights.

(l. to r.) Panici, Sadus, Marshall, LoBue, Gliottoni

We did it because our citizens had been burdened year
after year with a water system that relied on wells dating
back to the city's early days. The water was awful! It was
muddy, full of minerals like iron and manganese, barely
drinkable. Many would come right out and call it
undrinkable. For years the city had to treat that water
with a chemical called Tri-Lux. The material was at first
supplied, at prices later found to be inflated, by a man
we are going to hear a lot about, Nick LoBue.

Our water pipeline project put an end to the Tri-Lux
scam. The pipeline brought fresh, clean drinking water
to our town. And that wasn't all. Our clean water supply

also brought a major tax paying manufacturer into our community, the Ford Motor Company. The water project was our greatest accomplishment as a city administration. It was a legacy that our commissioners and staff created for the community. Let me tell you something about the commissioners who worked with me in those years.

Louise Marshall, to my mind, is everything that was right in local politics. Without saying a word she conveyed a grace that demanded respect. She didn't just "talk the talk." She "walked the walk" as they say. I met Louise when we were putting together the slate of candidates for our first ticket. She was a Republican township trustee and although the city elections were non-partisan at the time, Louise was everything we were looking for. No black woman had ever before even attempted to run for office in Chicago Heights. It was a risk for all of us but we took the chance.

Chicago Heights was an ethnically diverse town. The neighborhoods were the same kind of melting pot that formed our country. We had African Americans, Italians, Poles, Greeks, Germans, Slovaks, Hispanics and everyone else, all living in the same town. But they were living their lives as separate communities. We set out to break down those walls and start pulling together as a community. Louise Marshall was a vital part of that.

I can honestly say that in the four terms we worked together I never heard anyone say one negative thing about Louise. She was special in too many ways to number, a difference maker who broke down walls of race and gender with an elegance we rarely see. Not only was she a strong woman; she was a strong black woman. She pioneered the ideal of equality at a time in this country when, to be honest, it wasn't easy.

Remember, those were the mid seventies, when the country was just starting to move forward with equal rights movements. Thirty years ago things were different. The country needed visionaries, reformers. And that was Louise; she was a difference maker.

Louise was a successful business women; for an elected official that was really unheard of. She was in the insurance business, a tough game for anybody in those days. Can you imagine being a black woman selling insurance in the sixties and seventies in this country? There's an old photo of Louise and myself, published in the Star newspaper, holding hands as we jumped off of the steps at City Hall. Talk about a picture being worth a thousand words! We were taking quite a chance, but the risk paid off.

Our only agenda was to make Chicago Heights a community where people of any race, creed and gender could be proud to live. And together we succeeded.

Louise Marshall was a difference maker. My son Chuck knew Louise Marshall for twenty years. It would have been easy and proper for him to address her as Louise, but he said it never felt right. He always called her Mrs. Marshall because that was the kind of respect that she inspired.

And then there's John Gliottoni, "Johhny G." as people called him back then.

My father used to tell me that A&G Construction was the best contractor in Chicago Heights, and also the most expensive. John Gliottoni and his brother Andy owned the business. They earned the reputation of being the finest in their trade, and not being afraid to charge for it. My father was not an easy guy to satisfy when it came to the construction business. If you got his approval you had to deserve it.

I got to know John Gliottoni when I was president of the Chicago Heights Park District. John was on the board of Chicago Heights School District 170. We shared a lot of the same goals in forming a coalition ticket that would make Chicago Heights a community we could be proud of. John was a lifelong resident of the town and he really had the ability to get out the vote.

Johnny G. was a big guy with a soft heart who could light up a room when he walked in. Everybody loved him. I can still see him with his cigar in his hand, working a room, shaking hands with everyone and making everyone feel like they mattered to him. Because they did.

John never had a harsh word to say about anybody; he gave everyone the benefit of the doubt. He and I worked together for almost twenty years before he passed away in 2007. One of the hardest things I've had had to deal with was John's passing. Almost as hard was when we were both convicted and were forbidden to contact each other because of the felony laws. So here we are, two guys going through the most difficult time imaginable, two guys who had almost daily contact, who built a legacy together. And we were forbidden to even write to each other for almost ten years.

But you know what? Our friendship stood the test of time. When we finally were able to get together again it was as if time had stood still. We picked up right where we left off, just two old friends who wanted to make a difference in the community we were raised in. Johnny always told me to let this thing go, but he probably knew me better than anybody. He knew someday I would tell the truth about our ordeal, how a few careerists in the federal government conspired to bring down our administration. John knew I would tell the story for the sake of our families and never give up till I did.

John Gliottoni and I shared the same family values. Family was everything to John. In fact I still have breakfast with his son Joey once a week. Joey now runs the family business that his father started and it makes me proud to be able to call him my friend, just as I was proud to call John my friend. You see, where I come from those are values much more important than money and greed, the relationships that can stand the test of time and adversity. Those relationships matter more than all of the money in the world.

John and I always tried to do the right thing for Chicago

Heights but we didn't always agree on how to do it. I can remember arguing with him over something and he would laugh this infectious laugh and say "Come on Charlie. Please, let's just get it done right."

John and I used to drive the neighborhoods of Chicago Heights on Saturday mornings after we had breakfast, with a tape recorder. We would record notes about anything we saw that needed attention. Then we'd get a report out on Monday mornings to the heads of the street department, police and fire departments, water department and so on. The city employees couldn't believe how much we knew about what was going on in the city. But really it was just two guys driving around town trying to get it right.

I can still hear Johnny laughing that infectious laugh and saying, "Come on, Charlie. Please, let's get it done right".

We never had a problem that we weren't able to solve together and you know what? We did. At least we thought we did. I'm reminded of the time when the FBI approached us about brothels that were being operated in Chicago Heights at the time. John was our commissioner of public safety, so we asked the FBI for the help.

Help was not what we got! Far from helping us, they charged us a few years later with being a part of organized crime. Neither of us really understood at the time how that happened. Later it became perfectly clear. John Gliottoni, Louise Marshall and I together accomplished some great things for Chicago Heights and yet the best the government could do when we asked them for help was fabricate a case against us.

In 1979 there was no question that our team would run for a second term. However we needed a fourth candidate for city council. That was when we invited Nick Lobue to join our ticket. He had been a park board commissioner, and seemed to be a good, solid young business owner. Being Sicilian he had the potential to carry the Sicilian vote, which was an important segment of our electorate.

Chicago Heights was a very diverse community and people voted for candidates that they could relate to as much as they voted for the platform. In those days we didn't seriously vet candidates. It was as much a gut decision as anything. We did go so far as to run criminal background checks and of course we relied on the court of public opinion. Nick Lobue had no criminal record and he seemed well liked and respected in the community.

Little did I know that this was the guy who would one day declare his ambition to become "the first Mafia mayor " of Chicago Heights. None of us had any idea in 1979 that this guy would turn out to be the most corrupt extortionist the government had ever encountered. Even the federal prosecutor who made LoBue's lies the backbone of his case had to admit LoBue was "spectacularly corrupt." And nobody seemed to notice that when his lies were challenged in cross-examination LoBue answered, "I don't recall" no less than 850 times.

People have asked me more times then I care to recall, "How did you not know what was going on?" The best comparison I can make comes, it so happens, from the boyhood home of the late President Ronald Reagan, Dixon Illinois. It turns out that Dixon has the same commission form of municipal government that Chicago Heights had in our day. There's a part time mayor and four part time commissioners, pretty much the same set up.

Well, it turns out that Rita Crundwell, the comptroller who managed the finances of this small town of Dixon, embezzled municipal funds to the tune of $53,740,394 over a twenty-year period. That's equal to about one half of the town's entire budget. Yet nobody knew it was going on! It wasn't until a substitute accountant covering Ms. Crundwell's vacation stumbled across her secret bank account that the scheme finally unravelled. So when the FBI eventually approached the administration and asked the mayor for help and he fully cooperated. He helped them apprehend the embezzling comptroller.

How different that is from our case, when we contacted the FBI to help combat organized crime in Chicago Heights, only to see them try to associate us with it! That's right. Here I was, asking the FBI to join forces with us and help us get something done. I made it clear that I was a good mayor but that I was not the police. That was their job. Maybe they took it the wrong way.

Eleven years later, when I finally found out what LoBue had been up to and he was indicted on all of those charges, the government could have come to me and asked for my help. I would have gladly provided help, just as the Mayor of Dixon did. It was not until Lobue was indicted in 1990 that I became aware of his criminal activity. His goals were much different from mine. He was working on becoming a Mafia mayor; I was working to make Chicago Heights an all American city. While LoBue was shaking down contractors I was working to annex the Ford Motor Company into Chicago Heights.

Maybe it's time for me to show you some of the highlights of my career as a politician.

Chapter Four
The Rewards Of A Life In Politics

It was looking like just one more busy day at city hall.
But then everything changed.

Thelma, my secretary, shouted from the outer office,
"Chuck! ... Governor Reagan is on the phone and he
wants to talk to you."

"Sure," I thought, " and the Pope wants me have coffee
with him right after that." So I told Thelma to quit
messing around, that I had a lot of stuff to do today. But
she insisted.

"No really! It's Governor Reagan himself. He wants to
talk to you now!"

Things were going well during that first term of our
administration. We were getting recognition at levels
that I had never expected. In the spring of 1980 the
whole nation was focused on the upcoming presidential
election. I was named a delegate to the thirty-second
Republican nominating convention to be held in July at
the Joe Louis Arena in Detroit.

As a delegate I had given my commitment to Governor John Connally of Texas, the same Governor Connally who was in the car with President John F. Kennedy on that fateful November day in Dallas in 1963. But it was not Governor Connally on the phone; it was somebody I had never expected to hear from. It was the legendary ex-governor of California, the man who had very nearly defeated Gerald Ford for the Republican nomination in 1976.

I had to compose myself for a minute. Then I picked up the phone and said, "Governor, this is Chuck Panici. I can't tell you what an honor it is to hear from you. How can I help you?"

He said, "Mayor Panici, I have heard a lot about the success you and your organization are having in the South suburbs. We could use your help. Would you please consider being a delegate, representing me at the convention from your area?"

I was blown away. A call from Ronald Reagan to ask a favor of me! Not a call from his staff. A call from the man himself. What would my father say about that? This was a call from a man who could be president of the United States. I would like to be able to say that I remained calm and kept my cool, but I have to be honest.

I felt a sense of power come over me. He surely wasn't calling every potential delegate. Why me? He must have recognized our success, how we were able to get the vote out. I knew the reach was local, maybe even regional. And but I never thought the reach was national. Who wouldn't feel a sense of power?

I wanted to be cordial but I also had to be quick and honest with my answer. "I'm honored that you would call me directly and ask me to represent you," I said, " but I have already committed to John Connally. And I can't break that commitment, Governor. I want a strong ticket and between you and John, whoever is the candidate, we can't lose. The party can always count on my support."

He was disappointed but he said he was grateful and appreciated my honesty. And he wished me luck. As you can imagine, I had mixed emotions when I hung up from that call! This was a true test of what I considered my word and my commitment.

I was immensely excited by the phone call. And how could I have known that this would not be my first opportunity to be of service to Governor Reagan? Next time it would be to the 40th president of the United States, Ronald W. Reagan.

But between those two landmarks in my career as a politician there were lots of other peaks and valleys. I would find myself meeting, working with and befriending men and women who would have far reaching effects on my life and on the life of our country.

One such person was George M. O'Brien, a Republican Party colleague who was elected to the Illinois House of Representatives in 1971, at the time when I was becoming active in politics. In 1973, after only one term in the State House, George ran successfully for federal office. He became Representative for the 17th congressional district of Illinois.

Ten years older than me, Congressman O'Brien was a World War Two veteran. That experience might explain what I considered to be one of his great talents, the ability to see more than one point of view at the same time. Like me, he was often able to find the win-win solution to a tough problem. George O'Brien was one of those moderate Republicans who was able to win the support of Republicans and Democrats alike.

About the same age as George O'Brien was another Republican Party veteran who influenced my career. Ed Derwinski served twelve terms as U.S. Representative for the 4th congressional district of Illinois, representing the south and west suburbs of Chicago from 1959 till 1983. Congressman Derwinski was a World War Two veteran, like George O'Brien, who had served in the Pacific conflict and in the post-war occupation of Japan.

When he and I first met, Ed Derwinski was the ranking member of the House Foreign Relations Committee. He had also been a U.S. delegate to the United Nations and chairman of our delegation to the Interparliamentary Union. It was one of those ironies of politics that in 1982 these two leading G.O.P. flag bearers, George O'Brien and Ed Derwinski, found themselves running against each other in the Republican primary for the new 4th congressional district.

It was the Democrats who caused the problem. Following the national census of 1980 the Democrat House voted to redistribute the congressional districts so as to give the voters better proportional representation in Congress. The result was a dismemberment of the former 4th district that left Derwinski and O'Brien competing for election in the same, newly redefined 4th district! The way it worked out, there were more O'Brien than Derwinski supporters in the new district. So it was George O'Brien who went back to Washington after the 1982 mid-term election.

But ex-Representative Derwinski didn't suffer from the outcome. Knowing his abilities and experience President Ronald Reagan, halfway through his first term in the Whitehouse, put Ed Derwinski to work as a counselor in the State Department. In 1987 he was appointed Under Secretary of State for Security Assistance, Science and Technology. And there he remained, a key member of the administration team, for the rest of the Reagan presidency.

During the early seventies I had the opportunity to meet and work with another important political figure, Republican Party National Committee Chairman George H.W. Bush. My recollection of the elder George Bush is that he was the complete political pro. He was an ideal candidate when he first ran for Congress in 1967. A veteran of the South Pacific war, he had flown 58 missions as a navy pilot. He was a successful businessman who rose high in the Texas oil industry in the 1950s. Then he ran successfully in 1967 for the House of Representatives.

After a term in Congress he became President Gerald
Ford's Chief Liaison to China. In 1976 and 77 he served
as Director of the Central Intelligence Agency. After
that, of course, he became first a rival nominee and then
vice-presidential running mate of Ronald W. Reagan in
the 1979 race for the Whitehouse. And finally in 1988,
after slugging it out with Democrat Michael Dukakis in
a hard fought election, George Bush the Elder won the
presidency with 54% of the popular vote.

Meanwhile back in Chicago Heights there eventually
came another busy day at city hall when I heard Thelma

shout out, as she usually did, "Chuck! Governor Thompson wants to talk to you!"

It wasn't unusual for the governor to call. We had a good relationship. It goes back to when he was elected to his first term in 1976 when our organization was just starting to pick up steam. He always counted on Bloom Township to bring in the numbers for him.

Before he became Governor Jim Thompson was a U.S. Attorney in the Northern District. Probably his biggest case was the conviction of Otto Kerner, the 33rd governor of the State of Illinois. He prosecuted Kerner on bribery charges connected with betting scandals in the racetrack industry.

Thompson obtained a conviction in that very high profile case. Many people would say that it put him on the map. As a U.S. Attorney Jim Thompson didn't concern himself with which political party you were from. He was tough on both sides. They called him "Big Jim" Thompson because he stood six feet six inches tall. You can imagine the effect on the members of a jury when a lawyer that tall stared down at them to commence his opening argument!

The physical appearance might have been intimidating
but the real Jim Thompson was very personal when
making a point. He was destined for greater things than
US Attorney. He knew how to handle crime in in the
Chicago area, but he wanted to make a difference at the
state level. So with a little encouragement and promises
of support, he decided to throw his hat in the ring as
Republican candidate for Governor of Illinois in 1976.

I felt honored when he called me back to tell me of his
intentions. Of course he knew that my organization was
capable of being a real asset to him. We would work
really hard to put him in the governor's chair in
Springfield. He would go on to be the longest serving
governor of the state of Illinois. When he decided to run
for a third term, he made the announcement at the 3 Star,
our family's business on Hungry Hill. All the Chicago
Media were there: TV, radio, the press. Who would
have thought it possible to see such a thing happen in the
old neighborhood? It was a proud and humbling
moment for me.

So now I picked up the phone and said, "Governor what can I do for you?"

He said, "Chuck, we have to make this quick. We have a bit of a challenge and I need your help <u>now</u>."

"The president has scheduled a trip to the Chicago area and he's had to change his plans. He wants to come to Chicago Heights. They're giving us three days to put it together! Can you put something together in three days? You'll have all the support you need and I have the budget to make it happen. Chuck the president needs our help. Can we count on you?"

And before I even realize what the governor was saying, I answered, "Sure!" I didn't know what I was letting myself in for. I didn't anticipate the army of Secret Service agents, FBI, the advance team from Washington and the team from the governor's office.

Everyone who was going to have personal contact with the president had to undergo a background check by the Secret Service. I started putting together a list. We were to host a lunch in honor of the president, so it was up to me to decide who was going to join the President of the United States for lunch! And that's a lot tougher job than you might think! I didn't want to leave anybody out and yet I couldn't include everyone.

One of the people I had to leave off the list was my son Joe. At that time Joe wasn't all that into the political stuff so when he asked about it I told him I didn't think he would be interested. "Pop!" he said, "This is the president of the United States!" We still laugh about it to this day. My other son, Chuck Jr., still proudly displays the photograph of himself shaking hands with the president.

We held the presidential lunch in the cafeteria of the Bloom High School. We put together a group of community leaders who represented the culture of Chicago Heights. Leaders from the Italian, Black, Polish, Hispanic and Greek communities all gathered at the high school where we had all graduated just a few years before. It was a proud moment not only for me but for all of us, and for all that we had accomplished working together as a community.

I often wonder that with all the detail work that went into that day, all the background investigation, security planning and all of the safeguards that were put in place, not one problem was found; no scandal, no hint of corruption. Whereas only a couple of years later ... well, we'll get to that soon.

The plan called for a group of Blackhawk helicopters to fly the president's party from O'Hare Airport and land in a field by the high school. We had to build a walkway from the landing area to the high school entrance. And we had to prepare the school's cafeteria for the group luncheon with the president. Everything was happening so quickly that I couldn't even stop to realize what was actually happening.

The president of the United States was coming to Chicago Heights for a visit with me and my staff. He would give a speech on tax reform, the policies that would later become known as Reaganomics. And the speech would be broadcast all over the world. Think about it!

"And now from Chicago Heights, a south suburb of

Chicago, here is the president of the United States!"

I have had important visitors but nothing to compare with this. And I don't think anything ever will. My next thought was about my father. I would have given anything for him to be there - and maybe he was, with that look on his face, "Hmm! That's pretty good. Look who's coming to see my son!"

And I have to say that I'm as proud of my team as my father would have been of me. It's hard to believe that it all happened in three days. We had plenty of support from the governor's office. Traffic control and local and national media relations were two of the big jobs. In many ways it was like the old days when the circus came to town. That was when 1400 people and all the equipment would come to town on a train, set everything up including several tents and the Big Top, give a two and a half hour show, stay the day and then pack everything up and move on to the next town.

During an event like this every politician and public official wants to be seen shaking hands with the president and, if possible, get a picture. That's a big deal, having your picture taken with Ronald Reagan, a president who may go down as one of the most important in history. All the national and many of the International media were there, so we saw many faces familiar to us from television.

Finally the big day arrived. The whole place came alive. Everyone knew something special was going on. They closed off the 294 tollway from the Airport, blocking off all the local traffic. But the thing that really blew us away was when the five Blackhawk helicopters landed, and how all the people on board all got off at the same time so that it was impossible to tell which one was carrying the president. Those secret service people really knew their business!

As we waited at the school to greet the president a strange thought came to mind. " I wonder if his hair really is that black?" In a few minutes I had my answer. He came up to shake my hand and I saw that his hair really was black and healthy looking. That was when I thought, "Oh, boy! Maybe I should have accepted the offer to be his delegate when he called me before the nominating convention!"

To Mayor Charles Panici With best wishes, Ronald Reagan

Our official party waited in the hallway of the school
with the Secret Service, the police and all the
unbelievable security. And as the president came in,
who should run up to him with a big hug but my wife,
Dolores - one of the few women who could have gotten
away with it! Not only was she the first lady of Chicago
Heights; she was also the first lady of Chicago Heights
ever to hug a president. And as I looked on, with a bit of
anxiety, I was relieved to see that our president was in
fact the gentleman I thought he was. He smiled,
returned my wife's big hug with an equally big hug of
his own and said, "Good to meet you." Then he turned
and shook hands with me.

70

Dolores told me later that he had the softest hands of any politician she had ever met, and she had shaken hands with many politicians! She had never met any politician like him, she told me later, nor anyone at all who was quite like him.

After he and I had shaken hands I asked, "Well, Mr. President, what would you like to do?"

"Let's have lunch," he said.

So in we went to the private area adjoining the cafeteria, sat down and had a really nice lunch. There was no heavy discussion of political topics, just small talk. The president was relaxed and cordial. I did ask him one question. Noticing that the photographers, reporters and video cameras had us surrounded like the Indians in a wild west movie, I asked, "Mr. President, how do you handle the media?"

He said, "Watch!" Then he made a little gesture to someone on the sidelines. It was like magic! Just like that, the media were asked to leave. Wow! How I wished

I could do that! When I mentioned that our hard working volunteers would appreciate having their pictures taken with him, President Reagan was more than gracious. "Whatever you want," he said.

So after the lunch and the speech were over, he stayed with us and posed for pictures with our volunteers. What a visit! What a memory! People are still talking about it - the day the president came to Chicago Heights!

Chapter Five
A Real Case and a Hypothetical One

I've mentioned more than once that I and two honest, hardworking colleagues were the victims of an unjust indictment and a rigged trial. There were two reasons why we suffered that injustice. The first was to save the skin of a would be mafioso big shot, Nick LoBue, who was facing a lifetime behind bars on racketeering charges. The second was to further the ambitions of justice department lawyers and FBI agents. I am now going to explain just how the interests of this junior "wannabe" gangster and these ambitious justice department employees happened to coincide.

But first I want to show you some facts that explain why the government was unable to build an honest, factual case against Chuck Panici, John Gliottoni and Louise Marshall. There was no evidence against any of the three defendants. The entire prosecution was based on the untruthful testimony of four witnesses, Nick LoBue, Ralph Galderio, Donald Prisco and Rodney Costello. All were themselves guilty of "predicate" crimes under the RICO Act, some more serious than others. All four were bribed with the promise of leniency if they cooperated and coerced with the threat of heavy prison terms if they didn't. When prosecutors get people cornered in that position, very few will refuse to say whatever they're told to say on the witness stand. So it was that these four birds all got up and sang the song the government told them to sing. But as we'll see, several were out of tune with each other and a couple were tone deaf.

And why is it that the federal prosecutors were unable to bring any kind of *prima facie* evidence proving beyond doubt that the three accused had committed crimes? Simple. There exists no such evidence because the three defendants committed no such crimes. And why did Nick LoBue suffer from that strange "selective amnesia" whenever he was cross-examined? 850 times he answered, "I don't recall."

For myself, I had no motive to solicit bribes or kickbacks. I didn't need to. I was making good money as an honest businessman. Compared with the lawful income I was earning, the kickback payments alleged by the government would have been chicken feed. They totaled well below $25,000 a year. During those years I was filing tax returns showing average annual income of

$225,000 a year. All those kickbacks I was accused of receiving would have added maybe 10% to my annual income. Do you know of any sensible businessman who's willing to risk disgrace and imprisonment just to add 10% to his income? I don't either. Certainly neither I nor John Gliottoni nor Louise Marshall was stupid enough to risk so much for so little.

Now Rita Crundwell is another story altogether. She's the former comptroller of that small city of Dixon, Illinois, boyhood home of President Ronald Reagan. Ms. Crundwell took a big chance when she started intercepting municipal checks and siphoning them off into her own secret bank account. But Rita figured the payoff was worth the risk. She stole more than 53 million of the taxpayers' dollars over a period of 20 years.

Two and a half million dollars a year! That's big money by anybody's reckoning. But she got caught and she's paying the price. Rita Crundwell was convicted of wire fraud and embezzlement in 2012.

She will spend the "golden years" of her life behind bars. That's the way it goes nearly every time. Either they run away into exile in Brazil or it's life behind bars. Would we three have thought we were any different?

But the case of Dixon, Illinois in 2012 is vastly different from Chicago Heights, Illinois in 1990. First and foremost, the government people who handled the Dixon case were not the same people. In Dixon the FBI approached Mayor James Burke, alerted him to the problem and asked for his cooperation, which Mayor Burke was glad to provide. Working together they uncovered the embezzlement and brought the perpetrator to justice.

Chicago Heights in 1990 was totally different. Maybe it was the Italian surnames involved, or maybe the big Democrat machine was hoping to sabotage our little Republican machine. Maybe – and this is probably the real scenario - it was just that a small time crook and some ambitious government employees saw the chance to scratch each other's backs for fun and profit. Whatever the case, when the FBI approached Mayor Chuck Panici and the city commissioners they weren't asking for cooperation the way they did in Dixon. They were seeking indictments.

And that's not all. Not only did they indict the mayor and two of the city's four commissioners. They dropped all their RICO *(Racketeer Influenced and Corrupt Organization)* charges against the real perpetrator, wannabe gangster politician Nick LoBue, when he volunteered to lie for them on the witness stand.

How would that story have gone if it had been Chicago Heights in 1990 instead of Dixon in 2012? The FBI would have arrested Rita Crundwell and the Justice Department would have indicted her just as they did in Dixon. But if it had been Chicago Heights in 1990 Rita would have asked for a plea bargaining deal. And they would have given it to her.

"If you charge Mayor James Burke with embezzlement and wire fraud and reduce the charges against me," Rita tells the federal prosecutors, "I'll testify that Mayor Burke and I were in cahoots together with two city commissioners and he was the master mind behind the whole scheme."

And the prosecutors say, "Hey! that's a good idea. Rita Crundwell alone is small potatoes. She's just a 58 year old bookkeeper that nobody cares about. Convicting her and putting her in jail won't make a big splash in the media. But if we can nail the mayor and maybe even some of the city commissioners on corruption charges - now that's a case that will make headlines! We'll all get promotions. Some of us might even get to be judges."

Of course analogies are never exact. To make the Dixon case parallel Chicago Heights they would have to catch some smaller fry with their hands in the till. They would need to find people who collaborated with Rita Crundwell. Those people could then be threatened with terrible prison sentences unless they agreed to testify against Mayor Burke and his commissioners. And, though I hate to say it, they would have needed some Italians in the picture with real or imagined mob connections.

Grotesque? Unprincipled? Dishonest? Certainly. But that's the way the United States Department of Justice was winning cases in Chicago early in the 1990s. In a coming chapter I'll show you how they went about it. I'll expose and analyze the nasty tricks they played on the justice system. The success of their conspiracy did win them advancement, and one of them actually did become a judge. And the real crook, Nick LoBue, walked! Crime can pay handsomely sometimes, if you're on good terms with the right people in the Justice Department.

Chapter Six
Prosecutorial Misconduct:
"Win at all Costs!"

I mentioned earlier my reason for writing this book. I'm
not seeking revenge on anyone. I'm not questioning the
laws we live by. I'm not looking for a new trial. I don't
expect the Justice Department of the United States to
change its mind about my case or those of my friends
and colleagues, Louise Marshall and John Gliottoni.

What I do hope for is a review of our case in the **Court
Of Public Opinion**. I'd like the public to clear my name,
and the names of my two fondly remembered colleagues,
both sadly now departed. And I think you will vote for
acquittal, once you know the facts.

In any criminal case, including ours, the prosecution
supposedly bears a certain "burden of proof." They're
required to prove their case "beyond a reasonable
doubt." In our case they came nowhere near proving
their allegations beyond a reasonable doubt. How could
they? They had no evidence. All they had was an
elaborate fiction, and a chorus of lies to make it seem
convincing. But with a clever game of show-and-tell,

which the media blew up into a widescreen epic, they persuaded the jury to buy it.

A moment I can never forget was when the one of the prosecutors in our trial, a man named Chris Gair, declared in his final argument to the jury, "The city in which all these crimes took place may be the most corrupt city in the whole United States."

Talk about gall! Talk about chutzpah! Talk about Improper Argument! A fair and vigilant judge like Andrew Napolitano – whose views we're going to read about very soon - would have halted Gair on the spot for that attempt – a very successful attempt - to inflame the jury against the defendants. At the very least the remark should have been struck from the record and the jury cautioned to ignore it. Ethical lawyers shudder at that kind of rhetoric. But the man on the bench at our trial was James B. Zagel, whose career as a lawyer is unusual. He was never a defense lawyer. He worked only as a prosecutor. Zagel was also Director of the Illinois State Police for seven years. This explains Zagel's strong (and perhaps unconscious) bias in favor of the prosecution. What others see as judicial abuse of discretion may be to him no more than seeing justice done. Supreme Court Justice Sonia Sotomayor warns against this kind of unconscious bias.

Every judge comes to the bench with personal experiences. If you assume that your personal experiences define the outcome, you're going to be a very poor judge, because you're not going to convince anybody of your views. You have to be a judge that is able to step aside and determine when their personal bias is influencing the way they're thinking about a case. You're not a very good judge if you're incapable of that. And, in fact, I have spoken previously about the fact that, as judges, we have to be sensitive to that. We have to know those moments when our personal bias is seeping into our decision-making. If we're not, then we're not being very good judges. We're not being fair and impartial.

It was Judge Zagel who in hearing the trial of former Illinois Governor Rod Blagojevich made disputed calls that may yet get Blagojevich's conviction overturned on appeal. The appeal says Judge Zagel admitted questionable testimony against Blagojevich and excluded evidence that tended to exonerate him. The Chicago Tribune wrote about it on June 28, 2011.

The appeal will likely argue that in both trials, the judge unfairly barred the defense from playing many undercover recordings critical to its case, severely limited cross-examination of government witnesses and allowed too many jurors who professed bias onto the panel ...

I don't defend or condemn Rod Blagojevich. But I do note a visible pattern in James Zagel's behavior on the bench. His choice of what evidence to admit and what to exclude usually benefits the prosecution. Not the classic image of Lady Justice as a blindfolded woman holding a sword and scales.

With Zagel we saw the scales were skewed before our trial even started. According to the account of the *Huffington Post*, Blagojevich's attorneys saw the same thing. It was clear to them that Judge Zagel was in the prosecutors' pocket from start to finish. In hindsight I can see that I should have instructed my legal team to file a Motion to Recuse.

In defense motions filed during Blagojevich's retrial, the defense accused Zagel of bias, pointing to how he almost invariably sided with prosecutors when there were objections during testimony.

As we can see, this is a leopard that hasn't changed his spots! And again in the same report …

Blagojevich's lawyers also have complained that Zagel had repeatedly rejected their requests to play FBI wiretap evidence that they claimed would help their defense.

This bias repeatedly occurs in Judge Zagel's selection of what evidence to admit and what to exclude. This is where the invisible hand of a biased judge can steer the course of a trial in a chosen direction. The testimony of

84

the prosecution witnesses was not only uncorroborated. Often it was ridiculous. I'll give you some examples in the coming chapter that would be comical if the consequences were not so tragic.

I'm not exaggerating. There was no physical evidence of any wrongdoing by any of the three defendants. Certainly crimes were committed in Chicago Heights, but all the evidence points to the prosecutors' own witnesses: Nick LoBue, Ralph Galderio, Donald Prisco who with the guarantee of immunity, leniency and money, were happy to shift the blame for their crimes to the mayor and the two city commissioners. There was plenty of physical evidence to convict the prosecutors' witnesses. In her closing argument prosecutor Marsha McClellan had to acknowledge that fact. She was obliged to admit that there existed no physical evidence that any of the three defendants had received kickback payments or, for that matter, money in any form other than lawful business dealings.

"The money trail," McClellan had to admit, "ends with LoBue." This is the prosecution's star witness, the man who 850 times answered, "I don't recall," but nevertheless was somehow able to remember tiny little details when he wanted to. This is the guy who told the story of how he and Mayor Panici visited Mob boss Al Pilotto in prison but couldn't remember when the visit took place, what airline they flew with or what hotel they stayed in.

In order to win their case, the federal prosecutors had to get twelve jurors to ignore important facts and believe unproven allegations. That's hard to do, but the lawyers who acted for the Justice Department were experienced and skillful. They were very good at their jobs. Their motives were questionable, to put it mildly, but they did their work with skill and finesse. And the jury, after all, was a group of lay people who wouldn't have recognized *prima facie* evidence if it came up and bit them.

These prosecutors also had help, in court and elsewhere. There's a widespread evil in our nation's justice system. The technical term is "prosecutorial abuse." It refers to the improper and often unlawful methods that prosecutors are able to apply for the purpose of winning a conviction without regard for guilt or innocence. Forget about Justice, the blindfolded lady with the balance scales in one hand and the sword in the other. The goal of these methods is to win, no matter what.

Former Florida prosecutor **Robert Merkle** puts it in plain words. "It's a results oriented process today; fairness be damned." In other words, "We're going to put you in jail one way or another, by fair means or foul. Because we can. We're the government"

The same Wikipedia article that quotes US Attorney Merkle also quotes former Chicagoan **Francis Fukuyama**, the well known economist, political scientist and author of hefty books like *The End Of History And The Last Man*. Fukuyama puts a finger on Prosecutorial Misconduct and the problems it creates, problems like "... a distrust of government and the belief that public authorities are in a vast conspiracy to violate the rights of individuals." Fukuyama asserts that "such misconduct may actually be widespread in the United States."

I believe him, and with good reason.

Another critic of improper conduct among prosecutors is

the well known former New Jersey Judge **Andrew P. Napolitano**. During his years on the bench of the Superior Court of New Jersey Judge Napolitano repeatedly found prosecutors abusing their powers and acting improperly. He himself never allowed it, but other judges - even in the higher courts - have not been so scrupulous or so vigilant.

Now the popular chief legal analyst of the Fox Television Network, Judge Napolitano is a harsh critic of the dishonest things federal lawyers often do. In his best selling book *Constitutional Chaos* he writes, "Amazingly, infuriatingly, incredibly, the government will lie, cheat, and steal in order to enforce its own laws. And the courts continually give law enforcement a free pass to engage in these practices."

Federal prosecutors regularly break the law and pursue justice by lying, hiding evidence, paying for perjury and incriminating innocent people in order to win indictments and convictions. Rarely are these federal officials punished or even admit their conduct was wrong. Victims lose their jobs, assets, even families. Some go to prison because prosecutors withhold favorable evidence or allow fabricated testimony. Often the real criminals walk free as a reward for conspiring with the government to subvert the rights of others.

The Wikipedia entry on Prosecutorial Misconduct notes that, "Prosecutors are protected from civil liability even when they knowingly and maliciously break the law in order to secure convictions, and the *doctrine of harmless error* is used by appellate courts to uphold convictions *despite such illegal tactics*, thus giving prosecutors *few incentives to comply with the law*.

Tell me about it! More important, do you hear anyone in Washington denying it?

Here is a list of the abuses that unscrupulous prosecutors commit with no fear of reprisal:

* False confession
* False arrest -- abetting
* ***Falsified evidence***
* ***Intimidation***
* Police brutality -- abetting
* *Prosecutorial corruption -- always a possibility*

* Political repression
* ***Racial profiling***
* Sexual abuse
* Surveillance abuse -- abetting
* ***False testimony -- Subornation of perjury***

And here is a second list, also from the Wikipedia entry on Prosecutorial Misconduct, of the many abuses of privilege that prosecutors are able to, and often do, perpetrate:

* **Selective prosecution**, perhaps required for lack of resources, but potentially corrosive.
* **Capture of the grand jury**, misusing it as a tool for inquisitorial abuse, or excluding citizen complaints from being heard.
* **Plea bargaining abuses**, such as seeking testimony in exchange for leniency. This may solicit perjury or falsified evidence.
* **"Horsetrading"**, the practice of colluding with defense attorneys to agree to get some of their clients to plead guilty in exchange for letting others off.
* **Threatening public officials, *especially judges*,**

with prosecution if they don't unduly support their cases. (Is this why Zagel was so careful not to piss off the prosecutors?)

* **Tainting of jury pools** with public statements by prosecutors that are either inaccurate, exaggerated, unsupported by evidence or that could be inadmissible at trial, and such statements become widely promulgated by the media.

* **Prosecutors causing depositions in a related civil trial** which were likely to yield exculpatory evidence to be stayed until a criminal trial concludes without the benefit of that exculpatory evidence.

* **Prosecutors naming a host of "unindicted co-conspirators"** in conspiracy cases to intimidate potential defense witnesses with threats of retaliatory prosecution.

* **Prosecutors using their Peremptory Challenges** to remove from the jury anyone with relevant experience in the complex subjects of a trial. Defense attorneys often use similar tactics. Both attempt to prevent a juror's technical knowledge from interfering with the credibility

of their expert witnesses.

* **Prosecutors pursuing criminal penalties for selected industry practices** in Corporate America when regulatory intervention would be more appropriate. For example, prosecuting a mechanic for minor violations of the Clean Water Act rather than affording the opportunity for the mechanic to correct his error and pay the appropriate fines.

* **Prosecutors using multidefendant trials** to get defendants to turn on one another in the courtroom, as judges may be reluctant to allow separate trials in multi-defendant cases.

I hope you noticed the mention of the media as frequent collaborators in "promulgating unsupported evidence." When Louise Marshall, John Gliottoni and I were indicted the **Chicago Sun Times, the Chicago Tribune** and the TV stations convicted the three of us and put us behind bars before the jury got anywhere near a verdict. The federal prosecutors played the media like Paganini played the violin. Even respected columnists like Steve Neal were taken in and bought the prosecutors' story hook, line and sinker.

It was back in 1940 that President Roosevelt's Attorney General, **Robert Jackson**, warned the people of America to keep careful watch over their Department of Justice and especially over the lawyers whose duty it is to act on behalf of the people.

"The prosecutor has more control over life, liberty, and reputation than any other person in America. His discretion is tremendous. . . . While the prosecutor at his best is one of the most beneficent forces in our society, when he acts from malice or other base motives, he is one of the worst. . . . If the prosecutor is obliged to choose his cases, it follows that he can choose his defendants. Therein is the most dangerous power of the prosecutor: that he will pick people that he thinks he should get, rather than pick cases that need to be prosecuted."

I couldn't say it better myself. We can argue about the issue of "malice or other base motives." But there's no doubt whatsoever that our Federal prosecutors can "pick people they think they should get, rather than pick cases that need to be prosecuted." I've seen it done.

You may have noticed that some of the items on the list of prosecutors' abuses are in **bold type**. The bold type signifies an abuse that recalls the government's case against us. Let's go down the list so that you can form your own opinion.

Falsified evidence --- This is not to say that prosecutors Fred Foreman, Chris Gair and Marsha McClellan *intentionally* used false evidence in our trial, only that they chose to believe (or behave *as if* they believed) the untruthful testimony of Nick LoBue, Ralph Galderio and Donald Prisco. The prosecutors admitted to the court that their star witness, former finance commissioner Nick LoBue, had "lied all of his adult life." Without LoBue's lies, shifting the blame from himself to the mayor and two commissioners, the prosecutors had no hope of winning. Their whole case, and the fate of the three defendants, depended on the word of a lifelong liar.

Intimidation --- No doubt about this one! Clearly the government's principal witnesses were both bribed and coerced. But prosecutors in the United States have given bribery and coercion nicer sounding names. They now call them "plea bargaining" and "immunity." The feds had laid RICO charges against both LoBue and Prisco. Remember, RICO stands for "Racketeer Influenced and Corrupt Organization." They caught LoBue extorting kickbacks from city contractors, with the backing of Mob boss Albert Tocco, a big player in the Chicago Outfit. Tocco got a life sentence in 1990 for a long list of crimes (which, strange to say, didn't include the killing of the Spilotro brothers that I mentioned right at the beginning of this book). The feds also nailed LoBue for overbilling the city for services provided by companies he controlled.

The Justice Department had enough on LoBue to put him in prison for the rest of his life. And that's where he was headed. But he saw (or was offered) the chance to wiggle off the hook. He cooked up a rip roaring tale of a mob-ruled city and a corrupt mayor working hand in hand with the Mob. The game suddenly changed for Nick LoBue. The prosecutors, imagining the headlines, must have got stars in their eyes. They made LoBue the best offer he could have wished for. No lifetime in jail for him! He would get immunity from prosecution on the RICO charges plus a light, maybe even a suspended sentence on reduced charges. All he had to do was tell the same lies in court; testify against Panici, Gliottoni and Marshall. It doesn't matter what kind of fancy clothes you put on intimidation; it's still intimidation.

Racial profiling --- My co-defendant, Louise Marshall, was African American, but that was not what turned the jury against her. It was the ethnic identity of her two co-defendants. When we expand *racial* profiling to include *ethnic* profiling we find ourselves looking at the cornerstone of the government's case. In the minds of our three white Anglo-Saxon prosecutors, and in the minds of the WASP-owned media, "Chicago Heights" + "Italian" = "The Mob!" That was the story they told first to the media and later to the jury, which coincidentally was a "Dago-free" jury comprising not one Italian American. Their aim was to link two elected officials of Italian-American origin, John Gliottoni and me, with a notorious Chicago mob boss, our long-ago childhood neighbor Albert "Caesar" Tocco. Evidence? None! except of course the lifelong liar.

Subornation of perjury --- A heavy rap to lay on any attorney at law, much less a prosecuting attorney, a person sworn to uphold the law and bring wrongdoers to justice. The legal expression means *"persuading or forcing a witness to give untruthful testimony under oath."* The definition of this prosecutorial abuse doesn't say it's always willful and intentional "with malice aforethought." We have to consider that Foreman, Gair and McClellan may have stitched together their clever fabric of lies and half-truths in the sincere belief that they had uncovered a real conspiracy. Maybe they thought they had to stretch the truth - and sometimes create pure fiction - to get a conviction that was just and right but would have been beyond their reach if they relied on nothing but truthful testimony. But that's no excuse for suborning perjury. The rules of the American Bar Association are clear.

If the lawyer knows, from the client's clearly stated intention, that the client will testify falsely, and the lawyer cannot effectively withdraw from the representation, the lawyer must either limit the examination of the client to subjects on which the lawyer believes the client will testify truthfully; or, if there are none, not permit the client to testify; or, if this is not feasible, disclose the client's intention to testify falsely to the tribunal.

Golly! That doesn't leave much of a way out for our three Chicago prosecutors. In fact it leaves a twisty-turny puzzle in logic, doesn't it? If LoBue's stories were true, why could they not then or now produce any physical proof. Otherwise the three prosecutors must have been willing to believe a self-confessed lifelong liar despite the absence of any proof. But wait! There's a third possibility. Maybe they did, sort of, disclose LoBue's intention to lie as the rules required them to. Maybe that was why they made a point of characterizing him as a perennial liar. But they didn't warn the court that he was likely to lie. They painted LoBue as a perennial liar and thief who had suddenly begun to tell the truth. But only as much "truth" as they wanted him to remember. When he didn't have a lie ready for the defense lawyers, he replied, "I don't recall" 850 times.

Chris Gair, prosecutor, now defender

Unfortunately our lawyers missed a crucial chance to
impeach and discredit LoBue with the **Liar's Paradox**.
Don't feel bad if you haven't heard of the Liar's
Paradox. I didn't know about it either. It's an exercise in
logic where someone says, "This statement is false."
Seems pretty straightforward at first. But wait a minute.

If it's *true* that "this statement is false," then the
statement is actually *true* isn't it? The truthfulness of the
statement depends on it being false. But wait! If "this
sentence is false" is false, then the sentence is true,
which therefore means that it's actually false, but that
would mean that it's true … and so on into the
unimaginable future.

Here's an exchange that should have taken place early in

the trial..

"So, Mr. LoBue, you admit that you're a perennial liar. Then how are we to believe your account of sharing the bribes and kickbacks with your fellow commissioners?"

"That part is true. I did share those payments."

"Of course you did. But wait! You're a liar. So if you say you made those payments, and you admit to being a liar, then it's very likely that you did not in fact make those payments. Correct?"

"No, that's not correct! I didn't lie about that. I wouldn't lie about something that important."

"Then what did you lie about? When you say something, we have to keep in mind that it's as likely to be a lie as to be true. How can we know the difference?"

"Well, maybe I could sort of wink when I'm lying and not wink when I'm telling the truth."

"But that doesn't help us at all. You might well wink when you're not lying, and the other way around, just to mislead us. I have to say to you, *and to this judge and jury,* that we simply <u>can't rely on anything you say</u>."

Chapter Seven
Only One Problem - No Evidence!

There are good reasons why many of our United States no longer use the Grand Jury system. It's a system that unscrupulous prosecutors have found easy to abuse. You will soon see some examples of prosecutors using the grand jury process in ways that, putting it as fairly as possible, can be seen as misconduct.

The purpose of the grand jury is supposedly to determine whether the government ought to *indict* - that is, proceed to prosecute - some person or persons for an alleged crime. It's not the best way to make that decision, not by a long shot. To begin with, a grand jury is a captive audience for the prosecution.

And very often prosecutors literally do "capture" the grand jury. It becomes their private shooting gallery. The problem is that a grand jury proceeding is a one-sided affair. The prospective accused isn't present, nor is he or she represented by a lawyer. No opinions are heard other than those of the prosecutors. The second problem is that prosecutors are allowed to present *hearsay evidence* to a grand jury. There's no good reason for the process to be so one-sided, unfair, secretive and shoddy about evidence. It's just been that way for 200 years. In fact the grand jury system somehow manages to erase the rights we were guaranteed in the Sixth Amendment of our Constitution.

Grand juries - that is to say, panels of 12 to 23 people convened by the court to consider the evidence against a prospective defendant - were first formed in England in the 12th century.
Originally it was a group of ordinary people looking at evidence and quite often going out in person to find evidence of possible wrongdoing. But little by little it turned into the exclusive prosecutors' shooting gallery that we now have in our Federal Courts. To correct this unequal situation Britain and most of the other Common Law countries: Canada, Australia, New Zealand and many of these United States, have abandoned the grand jury process.

All of these jurisdictions have replaced the grand jury with a balanced and equitable legal proceeding known as a *preliminary hearing* or *pre-trial hearing*. The preliminary hearing avoids the flaws in the grand jury process. Prosecutors don't have a captive audience all to themselves. They have to present their facts and their evidence before a judge and it is a judge, not a group of laymen, who decides whether a suspect should be indicted. Because they are in a courtroom before a judge, prosecutors are obliged to comply with the legal *rules of evidence*. With very few exceptions those rules exclude the kind of *hearsay* evidence (another word for "gossip") that are freely admitted in a grand jury proceeding. And because defense attorneys are also present, the prosecution doesn't get away with the fast and loose talk that has become so prevalent in grand jury proceedings.

There was a lot of hearsay and half-truth in the federal grand jury proceedings that resulted in indictments against me and my two commissioners. In a modern day pre-trial hearing that kind of hearsay and half-truths would be challenged by the defense and very likely disallowed.

Here's *Wikipedia's* take on the flaws of the grand jury system. "The most persistent criticism of grand juries is that jurors are not a representative sampling of the community, and are not qualified for jury service, in that

104

they do not possess a satisfactory ability to ask pertinent questions, or sufficient understanding of local government and the concept of due process. Unlike potential jurors in regular trials, grand jurors are not screened for bias or other improper factors. They are rarely read any instruction on the law, as this is not a requirement; their job is only to judge on what the prosecutor produced. The prosecutor drafts the charges and decides which witnesses to call.

"The prosecutor is *not* obliged to present evidence *in favor* of those being investigated. Individuals subject to grand jury proceedings do not have a Sixth Amendment constitutional right to counsel in the grand jury room, nor do they have a Sixth Amendment right to confront and cross-examine witnesses. Additionally, individuals in grand jury proceedings can be charged with contempt if they refuse to appear.

"Furthermore, *all evidence is presented* by a prosecutor *in a cloak of secrecy*, as the prosecutor, grand jurors, and the grand jury stenographer are *prohibited from disclosing* what happened before the grand jury unless ordered to do so in a judicial proceeding.

"In 1974 the Supreme Court of the United States held in *U.S. v. Calandra* that the exclusionary rule in search-and-seizure cases does not apply to grand jury proceedings. *Illegally obtained evidence*, therefore, *is admissible* in grand jury proceedings, and the Fourth Amendment's exclusionary rule does not apply."

How is it that a country as devoted to fairness and the rule of law as the United States of America behaves as if we were still in the 18th century, when high justices in powdered wigs and scarlet robes decided whether common people lived or died depending on how they happened to feel about lunch? Is it any wonder that England, Scotland, Ireland, Canada, Australia and half of our United States have thrown out the grand jury with the rest of the antiquated constitutional garbage?

But antiquated as it is, unfair as it is, the grand jury system is what we still have in our federal courts. It's a system that perfectly suited the justice department prosecutors when in 1992 they sought indictments against Louise Marshall, John Gliottoni and myself. Cloaked in secrecy, managed (or manipulated)

106

exclusively by the prosecutors, exempt from the Sixth Amendment requirement to let the accused confront and cross-examine their accusers - it was a setup custom made for prosecutors to turn lies, half-truths and pure fiction into what looked like a conspiracy.

There really was a conspiracy. There never was any doubt of that. But the real conspirators: LoBue, Galderio, Prisco, Costello and the minor players, weren't on the list that went before the grand jury. They were the prosecution witnesses! The real criminals were happy to shift the blame for their crimes onto the mayor and two commissioners of the city they had robbed.

The case they wanted to build was a work of fantasy. They were alleging that the three prospective accused had somehow, within a ridiculously short time, become big players in organized crime. Their story was that we were not just organized criminals but had actually risen high in the "Chicago Outfit" - the local branch of the Mob. They didn't know, or more likely didn't care, that up till we resigned our elected positions in 1991, we were all earning a good, honest living. None of us had the time, even if we'd had the inclination, to pursue careers in the Mafia.

But it still wasn't easy for the prosecutors. Sure, the grand jury was their captive audience. They were able to present any bull-S story they liked under the cloak of grand jury secrecy. The accused weren't allowed to cross-examine the prosecution witnesses. We weren't even allowed to be present. They didn't have to obey the rules of evidence. They could even present evidence illegally obtained, or fabricated out of thin air, without anybody calling them on what they said or making them "show probable cause" which is supposedly the thing that determines whether the accused will be indicted.

But even with the dice so heavily loaded in their favor, the prosecutors didn't really have a case. They had no evidence. None! They had audited our books, pried into our bank accounts, followed us around town, bugged private conversations, wiretapped telephone calls - and they had come up with a big zero. They found absolutely no evidence of wrongdoing by Panici, Gliottoni and Marshall because there *was* no wrongdoing.

So they had to manufacture their evidence. In a country

108

like Scotland, prosecutors who fudged evidence the way our federal lawyers did would get shot down in flames at the pre-trial hearing. The defense lawyers would tear their case to shreds, the judge would throw it out and they'd be tarred, feathered and ridden out of town on a rail by their bar association.

But in US federal courts it's different. Here they can present to the grand jury a document called a "Santiago Proffer." "Santiago" you may remember is the patron saint of Spain but in this case it was the name of a suspect in whose drug trafficking case federal prosecutors first used this outrageous legal dodge. So what's this kind of "proffer?"

Well, it's a submission that when put into plain language, says, "We don't actually have sufficient evidence to indict these people. In fact, just between you and me, we *don't have any evidence at all*, because this is a conspiracy, see? And conspirators have this irritating way of keeping their doings secret. So instead of real evidence we're asking you to believe what these criminals are telling us. It's true that they are convicted criminals. It's also true that they can't prove what they say. All they can do is vouch for each other. It's actually just gossip. And they're only testifying because we've made a deal not to prosecute them for their own crimes. In return for that they have to say what we tell them to say. Unfortunately we can't offer you any *disinterested* witnesses - people who have nothing to gain or lose by their testimony - because *no such witnesses exist*.

So despite the fact that our case rests entirely on hearsay, the uncorroborated testimony of known criminals, we're asking you to accept their story *as if it were real evidence*."

I'm not pulling your leg. That's what a Santiago Proffer is. It's a request for the grand jury to pretend the cock-and-bull story of a bribed and coerced criminal is actually true. Bribed?Coerced? Certainly! What greater reward for a criminal facing life imprisonment than the promise of immunity from prosecution? What heavier coercion than the threat of long imprisonment if you don't say what they tell you to say? No less an authority than *Judge Andrew P. Napolitano*, the Fox Network's top legal expert, calls the plea bargaining immunity deal by its real name, *bribery*.

110

Now it is true that in those days the reputed boss of the Chicago Heights Outfit was a very tough guy named *Albert "Caesar"Tocco*, a guy a couple of years older than me, born and raised on the Hill, just a short distance from my home. Caesar was actually his middle name. Naturally Tocco and I knew each other. We were baptized in the same parish church; went to the same school. But that was about all the contact we had. Tocco didn't play basketball like I did. I doubt that many young, up-and-coming mobsters have time for basketball, except maybe betting on the big pro games.

So Albert "Caesar" Tocco was indeed a former neighbor and was, like me, of Italian origin. But you will remember me saying in the Foreword of this book that we had lots of Italian American neighbors in Chicago Heights, like Sam "Hobo" Cianchetti, the California Superior Court judge, and Dominic "Mimi" Falaschetti, the art teacher who was the first kid in our neighborhood to go to college. Maybe the feds were profiling? Maybe they had some formula that linked an Italian surname automatically with organized crime?

Anyway, the Chicago South Side Outfit was at that time doing the usual mix of legal and illegal businesses. They had "chop shops" where stolen cars were taken apart and stripped of their parts. They had whorehouses and call girl networks, drug distribution territories - but they also had legal businesses. A favorite Mob enterprise is "waste disposal" - garbage collection. Another is loan sharking, where working people can get an advance on their paychecks by paying interest rates well above what the law allows.

Some of these enterprises were located in Chicago Heights, but many more were in other parts of the Chicago Metropolitan area. Those Mob operations always go where the action is. And the Mob was certainly not new to Chicago Heights. They were there in the twenties and thirties, skimming their percentage off the bootlegging trade and operating their whorehouses. There are photographs of Al Capone and his pals taken in the Hungry Hill neighborhood.

Which is all well and good - but why were the feds trying to link the mayor and two other commissioners with organized crime? We were aware that organized

112

crime was active in our community. We knew they were always looking to buy the cooperation of city employees. That was why we asked both the police and the FBI for their help. We didn't get help. We got indictments.

Well, it turned out that there was a hidden logic to it all. What none of us knew was that our finance commissioner, Nick LoBue the Sicilian, was a closet Mafia wannabe. His secret ambition was to be the city's first mafioso mayor. And, again without our knowledge, LoBue was building a cozy relationship - or so he thought - with Albert "Caesar" Tocco, boss of the Chicago Heights Outfit. They were having regular breakfast meetings, doubtless discussing what ways a city commissioner might abuse his position - what they call "fiddles" in Britain - to siphon cash out of the city's coffers and into his own pockets.

LoBue and Tocco came up with one idea that was to cause them both so much trouble that later they must have wished they'd never thought of it. That was the garbage collection "fiddle," which we'll deal with in detail soon. LoBue developed other scams, frauds and kickback schemes. At least he said he developed them. I'm not convinced Nick LoBue was clever enough to dream up those kickback schemes. I think "Caesar" Tocco must have been his consultant. And on that point at least the feds agreed with me. They didn't think he was smart enough either. So between them they created the scenario that LoBue, the mayor and two of the commissioners were all in it together. According to their story, LoBue was siphoning kickback payments out of the city cashflow and splitting the take with Messrs. Panici, Gliottoni and Marshall.

That four-way split might sound like a promising theory at first. But when you look at the amounts of money involved, it falls apart. I mentioned in an earlier chapter that the sum total of the proceeds of all those crimes would have added about ten per cent to my income, and a smaller percentage to those of Johnny G and Louise Marshall. Not even a real crook takes the risk of breaking the law for that kind of chicken feed!

But neither the prosecutors nor the media took the trouble to figure that out. On February 3, 1993 the Chicago Tribune ran the heart-stopping headline,

"Chicago Heights Bagman Details Web Of Corruption!"
The reporter then demonstrates how little he knows.
"LoBue," he writes breathlessly, "himself a former
council member, allegedly passed along to the three
defendants, as well as previously convicted former city
officials, hundreds of thousands of dollars in bribes from
city contractors, sometimes in the form of cash wrapped
in paper bags, gold krugerrands from South Africa and
even municipal bonds."

The sums actually alleged against us were astronomical
but of course they couldn't be proven because they were
pure imagination. Actual evidence might have proven
seventy-five thousand dollars over a period of fifteen
years. Five thousand a year, supposedly split four ways
among the alleged conspirators. Golly! that's over a
thousand dollars apiece, $1,250 to be exact. During
those years I paid taxes on an average income of about
$225,000, honestly earned with my wedding
publications and hospital small accounts businesses.
Why would I bother? or Johnny G, or Louise?

It's a different story, though, when you ignore the
unlikely idea of the four-way split and put all the money

in Nick LoBue's pocket. That would more than double the income of our double dealing finance commissioner and of course the illegal portion is tax free. That way it does add up! And that, clearly, is the real story of the corruption that took place in Chicago Heights.

So again, why and how did the prosecutors cook up so improbable a case against the mayor and the two commissioners? My answer is a simple one that has the force of logic and fits all the facts. The feds had uncovered Nick LoBue's kickbacks scheme and found out what he had been doing. They had him dead to rights, together with several others: Ralph Galderio, Donald Prisco, Dante DeSantis, Rodney Costello and several others who were implicated. All were candidates for serious time behind bars. LoBue was good for a life sentence on the multiple RICO (Racketeer Influenced and Corrupt Organization) charges laid against him. That's what those breakfast meetings with "Caesar" Tocco had done for him.

But these were small potatoes. For an ambitious prosecutor, convicting those people was like putting the stuffed heads of a few muskrats on the wall of your trophy room. What they needed in order to make their names as crime busting heroes were some real trophy heads with lots of horns and antlers, like the mayor and a couple of commissioners. And here in their grasp was former finance commissioner Nick LoBue, an apprehended felon willing to say or do anything to avoid life imprisonment!

The possibility that must have really made the feds' mouths water was Nick LoBue's claim that he was not the only city official who was pals with Albert "Caesar" Tocco. What if the mayor and commissioners were in on the game too? What a feather in everybody's cap! Sensing that he just might avoid spending the rest of his life in the Joint and never at a loss for a lie, LoBue gave the feds a custom made whopper. He came up with his boldest lie ever, a tale of midnight meetings with the big boss of organized crime, an underworld conspiracy to take over the town. He painted himself as the trusted lieutenant of a mafioso mayor, in a plot to skim millions out of the public coffers.

It was pure imagination of course. There were no mafioso politicians, least of all Nick LoBue, who turned out never to have been more than a Mob groupie. Nor was there any proof to corroborate LoBue's stories. But his fable caught the imagination of the feds and for that reason it did actually save LoBue's skin. Prosecutors and FBI agents both saw their chance to hit the big time with a story that would make front page headlines.

And that, I'm satisfied in saying, was the basis of the conspiracy that followed. I don't expect you to take my word for it. I can show you the transcripts of the legal proceedings. I can   show you the transcripts of the *302s*, the FBI interviews with "persons of interest" that "may become testimony" in a trial. In those transcripts we see unfolding a growing fabric of lies and half-truths, orchestrated by people who had no reason to fear being accused of prosecutorial misconduct. We also see the conflicting details, the inconsistencies between one version of the story and another, that always show up when several people try to tell the same lie at different times.

They tell me it was the *Ivanhoe* guy, Walter Scott, who wrote those memorable words, "Oh, what a tangled web we weave: When first we practice to deceive!"

And what will we see at the end of this twisting and turning trail? No evidence whatsoever! No genuine evidence that any of the three accused ever committed a single unlawful act. Not even a parking ticket. All the prosecutors ever had, with all their bluster and courtroom oratory and news headlines, was the untruthful testimony of the witnesses they had seized by the throat, people who faced long, hard prison terms if they failed to say what the prosecutors told them to say.

The construction of this crime fiction began with the *302s*, the transcripts of interviews the FBI conducted with various "persons of interest" as they sought to build their case. And here's a question we ought to ask. Why are these interviews taken down in writing and presented to the courts in written form? Why are they not recorded? We've had voice recording technology for a hundred years and yet here's the FBI scribbling its own version of these interviews as if we were still back in the age of the quill pen and parchment paper.

I hate to say it, but I think you and I can both guess why. A written transcript can be edited, tampered with.

Inconvenient words can be taken out. Things can be inserted that were never said. In contrast a real time recording is hard evidence. The subject is heard speaking in his or her own voice. Sure, recordings can be messed with too, but audio edits are easy to detect. Not many people in the FBI or anywhere else have the fine editing skills it takes to "doctor" an audio recording into a credible forgery.

But the written word? No problem! Just write out a statement saying the things you want your victim to say and, with the threat of imprisonment, force him to sign it. When you have that kind of power, who needs evidence?

Chapter Eight
The Return of the *"Pathological Liar"*

From 1985 to 1990 one of our nation's favorite standup comedians appeared every week on NBC's sketch comedy program *Saturday Night Live*. Jon Lovitz created such comic fantasy characters as "Hannukah Harry," a Jewish contemporary of Santa Claus who lives on Mount Sinai and travels the world in a donkey cart giving unremarkable gifts to little Jewish boys and girls. An even more popular Lovitz character was "Tommy Flannagan, the Pathological Liar." This comically pathetic character used the catchphrase, "Yeah! That's the ticket!" as he laboriously completed his latest lie. One of his best was, "Married? Ah ...yeah, sure I'm married ... ah ... to ... um ... Scarlet Johansson ... who I've slept with. Yeah! That's the ticket." Or something close to that.

Jon Lovitz

Lovitz in 2008

Since 2001 Jon Lovitz has owned and operated the *Jon*

Lovitz Comedy Clubs in both San Diego and Hollywood. I haven't been able to visit either club and catch great standup comics like Russell Peters and Jon Stewart. I've been otherwise occupied. But it would be fun to see Jon Lovitz do his Pathological Liar routine again. It reminds me so much of Nick LoBue. So does the song Fred Astaire and Jane Powell sang in the 1951 movie *Royal Wedding*, said to be the longest song title on record, *"How Could You Believe Me When I Said I Loved You When You Know I've Been A Liar All My Life?"*

If I'm giving you the feeling that I harbor a dislike for Nick LoBue, that I consider him the lowest, most dishonest, most devious, slimiest sleazeball in living memory, then I must be successfully expressing myself. Nick LoBue admitted to the FBI that he had lied all his life. He admitted that he stole from his father, that he stole from his cousin, that he shook down contractors and public officials for bribes and kickbacks. And he went beyond that, although he didn't admit it, when he denounced honest friends and colleagues and threw them overboard as shark bait for the feds.

In a better legal system administered by sincere and honest people, LoBue's lies and treachery would be exposed and punished. But in the system we now have in our federal courts that kind of lying and scheming can not just get you off the hook; it can even reward you! Where's the justice in that?

The Founding Fathers of the United States of America created in 1776 the most original experiment in democracy that world had ever seen. They handed down to us a gift that we should never cease being grateful for - our Constitution.

But there was a cost. When the American legal system separated from the British Common Law it no longer evolved along with the law of the mother country. One way the American legal system stopped evolving was the one I mentioned earlier. British Common Law countries like England, Scotland, Canada, Australia and New Zealand got rid of the old grand jury process years ago. So did all but 22 of our 50 United States. The other 28 states have emulated the modern British process for seeking an indictment, the preliminary or pre-trial hearing. But in our federal criminal law the only way to seek an indictment is to go before a grand jury - a procedure that was permanently petrified in the Fifth Amendment.

As I tell you about the indictments, trial and conviction of Chuck Panici, John Gliottoni and Louise Marshall you will come to understand why the two biggest bees in my bonnet are (1) the Advocate Witness Rule and (2) the grand jury system. There are some others too, like the Brady Rule and the courts' baldfaced tolerance of Prosecutorial Misconduct. But those first two are the biggest and loudest.

In our case the federal prosecutors obtained their indictments purely and simply because they were able to take free advantage of a one-sided grand jury process. In the Superior Court of the State of Washington or the High Court of Scotland, prosecutors have to go up against their opponents, the defense attorneys. And they have to argue their evidence before a judge instead of 25 lay people. They have to comply with the rules of evidence. They can't offer hearsay as if it were authentic testimony. And if they can't show enough evidence to convince the judge that a suspect should be charged - "probable cause" in the language of our US courts, the prosecution ends right there. That happens more often than you might think.

But in the Northern District of Illinois, Eastern Division, of the United States District Court the prosecutors were free to present their custom made version of the facts without fear of contradiction. They didn't have to worry about proof. In our system the grand jury is the prosecutors' private shooting gallery. The *U.S. Attorney's Manual* states that prosecutors "must recognize that the grand jury is an independent body, whose functions include not only the investigation of crime and the initiation of criminal prosecution but also the protection of the citizenry from unfounded criminal charges."

What a laugh! The grand jury process is so antiquated, so arbitrary, so biased and so secretive that for prosecutors it's like shooting fish in a barrel. And that's how it was when they put their case against us, with their freshly prepared evidence and their bribed and coerced witnesses, before those 25 ordinary people. Most of them didn't know a tort from an apple turnover. It's the proud boast of that district division of the Justice Department that they "win 90% of their cases" and that they never prosecute a case unless they're sure the have "a 70% chance of winning."

In all fairness we have to remember too that in order to win all those cases they spend taxpayers' money like drunken sailors. There haven't been many cost effectiveness studies of the Justice Department's crime fighting efforts. But the studies that have been done so far show a seriously poor return on investment for the public purse. If Congress were to scale its funding according to the dollar efficiency of the Justice Department's district offices, a lot of lawyers and FBI agents would be in blue coats greeting customers at Wal Mart.

But back to our story. I guess everyone who has watched TV's "Law And Order" knows how the prosecution procedure goes. In a federal case it's the FBI that starts the ball rolling. They interview suspects, witnesses and "persons of interest" one or more times. Often they do these interviews over and over, hoping to catch the person in a lie. Lying to an FBI inquisitor - pardon me! - investigator, exposes you to the charge of *Obstructing Justice*. And once they've got that threat hanging over your head, they can squeeze you to "cooperate" with them. This can range from telling the truth, to stretching the truth, to bearing false witness to outright fabrication of untruthful testimony, depending on what the FBI and the US Attorney's prosecutors want from you.

Strange to say, these interviews are not voice recorded as they are in other common law countries. Instead the FBI writes them out in the form of "statements that may become testimony" on a form called a "302." The statements are not verbatim. The FBI doesn't want verbatim records of what is said. They want something they can "massage" a little. That way things can be inserted or omitted, numbers can be changed, dates can be revised. It's no different from the way the British "Bow Street Runners" operated in Charles Dickens' day when they handwrote statements, usually confessions, in pen and ink and turned them over to the "barristers" in their black robes and powdered perukes.

I explained earlier why this antiquated practice hasn't been replaced with modern voice recording equipment. It's like a crooked casino making millions on its craps tables with loaded dice. The only thing that can make them play fair is a higher authority like the gambling commission. But the US Justice Department is the highest authority. Who's going to make them change?

So this is the beginning of a prosecution. The FBI hands the 302 interview statements over to the prosecutors. If the prosecutors think they have a case they start building their documentation for a grand jury hearing. They don't have to use all of the 302 material. They can pick and choose. It all depends on what they feel it will take to get the bill(s) of indictment they're seeking.

And this is what happened in our case. Once they made the decision to believe Nick LoBue's story, or at least act as if they believed it, they wrote up their submission to the grand jury. In this and other aspects of their work these government lawyers showed a lot of skill and experience. They knew what would fly for them and what would not. As I noted in a previous chapter, they had no genuine evidence. All they had was some tame canaries, LoBue, Galderio, Prisco and Costello, who would say what they were told to say. But that was not enough. They needed to give the grand jury the appearance of corroborating proof.

They accomplished this by first presenting their version of the facts. This was an ingenious blend of half-truths and out-and-out lies. It began with LoBue's fiction of the corrupt mayor and commissioners working hand in hand with organized crime. According to LoBue he himself was just a tool in the hands of the master criminal Panici. He painted Panici as a tough guy who ruled Chicago Heights with an iron hand. Panici called all the shots, LoBue testified. When the mayor wanted a kickback for a city contract or a public works project, it was LoBue the "bagman" who went out and did the dirty work, collected the money and split the take among his fellow conspirators. And lurking in the shadows all the while, he told them, was the fearsome Al "Caesar" Tocco of the Outfit, friend and neighbor of both Mayor Chuck Panici and Commissioner John Gliottoni.

It makes a pretty good story until you take a close look.

It was the story that had got the prosecutors so excited. But LoBue on his own simply wasn't a credible witness. They had already nabbed him and charged him with a list of RICO crimes. They had also nailed Donald Prisco, former mayor of neighboring South Chicago Heights and business partner of Nick LoBue, on racketeering charges. And they had caught my secretary's husband, my old friend Ralph Galderio with his hand in the public till. In addition LoBue had implicated his cousin, Rodney Costello, in the RICO offenses. These were four people who could be persuaded to testify on behalf of the government. They could be coerced with the threat of "hard time" in the "Joint." They could also be bribed with the promise of leniency, even immunity from prosecution for their own offenses. All of them took the bait. Who wouldn't?

But even these four didn't add up to a case that might win indictments from the grand jury. Like LoBue, the three prosecution witnesses all had credibility problems. In Texas state courts they won't even listen to the testimony of a conspirator against another alleged conspirator, unless the conspirators' stories are backed up with authentic "smoking gun" evidence. It's no

130

surprise that they don't have that rule in a federal court. We've seen how the feds like to load the dice. But even so, four confessed felons all singing more or less the same song weren't going to get the feds anywhere near their 70% chance of winning.

But there's a way to get around that. Here's how they did it. There was ample evidence, both documents and witnesses, showing that crimes had been committed. For years Nick LoBue had been busy in Chicago Heights extorting bribes and kickbacks from contractors, engineering firms, consultants, even insurance agents. LoBue had even squealed on himself by cashing a $47,000 check, written to his company by an engineering consortium, through his own currency exchange business.

So the feds pulled a slick "Indian Rope Trick" with the evidence. First they presented their crime fiction story, then the rehearsed lies and half-truths of their bribed and coerced witnesses, and then finally a mountain of documents and witnesses proving that the alleged crimes did in fact take place. Doing it that way, nobody would notice that, although the crimes were real and there was ample proof of them, none of the hard evidence pointed to Panici, Gliottoni and Marshall. None of the other witnesses said things implicating the defendants. Some of them would give evidence at trial that tended to exonerate the three. All of the real evidence pointed to LoBue, Galderio, Prisco and Costello, the key prosecution witnesses. But that fact was lost on the 25 ordinary citizens of the grand jury, nor were any defense attorneys allowed to be present. Opposing lawyers would recognize and expose the prosecutors' sleight of hand.

This is exactly how the antiquated grand jury system deforms the process of justice, and how the modern pre-trial hearing prevents that kind of deformation. Can you imagine how the feds' motion for indictments would have gone in, say, a Washington State preliminary hearing? Not only would the defense attorneys recognize the trick the feds were trying to play; the judge, with his or her years of trial experience, would see right through it. The prosecution would crash and burn. The case would be thrown out.

That's what should have happened in Chicago. Instead,

like skilled stage conjurors the federal prosecutors misdirected the attention of their captive audience. The jurors saw what the prosecutors wanted them to see. They bought the whole story - lies, half-truths and facts all mixed up together - and dutifully handed down the indictments.

You think that's bad? It gets even worse in the next chapter.

Chapter Nine
Humpty Dumpty Justice: The RICO Act

"When I use a word," Humpty Dumpty said in a rather scornful tone , "it means just what I choose it to mean -- neither more nor less."

That's from Lewis Carroll's *Through The Looking Glass* where Alice has a talk with Humpty Dumpty, the famously accident prone character from Mother Goose. Alice's response is just as meaningful.

"The question is," said Alice, "whether you can make words mean so many different things."

Lewis Carroll was writing for children - or was he? His two **Alice** books, *In Wonderland* and *Through The Looking Glass*, are great entertainment for children and adults both, but they hint at deeper meanings too. In their absurdity the two stories expose and poke fun at the errors of human logic and the foolishness that follows. If our US Congress had been careful enough to read the *Alice* books in 1970 before it passed the **RICO** law, they would have realized what a Humpty Dumpty thing they were doing. And like all US presidents of the 20th century Richard Nixon had too much on his mind to notice the weird, open ended language of the bill he signed.

The *Racketeer Influenced And Corrupt Organizations Act* was actually a component part of the larger *Organized Crime Control Act*. The basic idea was good. In the 60s it was difficult to prosecute organized crime, often if was impossible. When **Robert Kennedy** took over as his brother's attorney general he began a serious campaign against the Mob. RFK's goal was not just to arrest and charge the ringleaders of the big Cosa Nostra families. He also wanted to flush the Mob out from behind the legitimate business fronts that so often hid it from view. The Teamsters Union, for instance, had a number of locals during the presidency of Dave Beck and his successor, Jimmy Hoffa, that were known to be controlled by the Mob.

Under RFK's leadership the Criminal Division of Justice Department had assigned a Special Attorney in its Organized Crime And Racketeering Section, **George Robert Blakey**, to go after the organized crime leaders, corrupt politicians and crooked union officials who had become such a thorn in the side of the Department. The campaign didn't last long. Following the assassination of President John F. Kennedy in 1963 Blakey left the public service and became a law professor at Notre Dame.

But in 1969 Blakey was back in Washington as Chief Counsel to the Senate Judiciary Committee's Subcommittee on Criminal Laws and Procedures. Working with the Subcommittee's respected chairman, **Senator John L. McClellan**, a Democrat from Arkansas, Blakey drafted what was to become the RICO statute. It was a dream come true for a former prosecutor. Time and again he had seen major Mob figures go free because their high priced attorneys were able to snooker cases out of court on technicalities. At long last he had a hand in drafting a new law that would eliminate those technicalities. In that effort Professor Blakey and Senator McClellan succeeded. In fact they succeeded too well.

The RICO Act didn't merely eliminate the technicalities that had been hindering federal Mob prosecutions. It went far beyond that. It eliminated the universal guarantee of due process that was spelled out in the Fourth Amendment of the Constitution. The language of the RICO Act gives our constitutional guarantees the kind of respect most of us reserve for toilet tissue. It was like going after the mice in your basement with a nuclear bomb.

William A. Fischel, veteran professor of economics and legal affairs at New Hampshire's Dartmouth College, gags and holds his nose at the "vague" and "almost meaningless" language Congress used in framing the RICO Act. Its open-endedness requires prosecutors to use maximum caution, he argues, to prevent the law from being misused in ways that Congress never intended.

The New York Bar Association, the governing body for practicing lawyers in the Empire State, also noted the salami-like qualities of Blakey and McClellan's RICO language. "The draftsmen of this bill," they said, "have made changes which sweep far beyond the field of organized crime." The New York lawyers' group found RICO's provisions had "not been adequately thought through." With furrowed brows they wrote that RICO "frequently hits targets which were not intended and misses those that were." Even more disturbing to the New York lawyers was RICO's "impatience" - a muted way of saying "runs roughshod over" - constitutional and procedural safeguards.

This outrageous open ended vagueness of the RICO statute takes us right back to *Alice In Wonderland*.

"I quite agree with you," said the Duchess; "and the moral of that is--'Be what you would seem to be'--or if you'd like it put more simply--'Never imagine yourself not to be otherwise than what it might appear to others that what you were or might have been was not otherwise than if what you had been would have appeared to them to be otherwise.'"

"I think I should understand that better," Alice said very politely, "`if I had it written down: but I can't quite follow it as you say it."

"That's nothing to what I could say if I chose," the

Duchess replied, in a pleased tone.

Without RICO the feds could not have prosecuted
Louise Marshall, John Gliottoni and me. They had no
other way of ruining the careers of three honest
politicians. In a fair trial, with the accused given all the
constitutional rights that keep prosecutors from loading
the dice against them the way RICO does, the feds' case
would have been thrown out for lack of evidence. I'll
show you how it works.

RICO was intended to give prosecutors an advantage in
dealing with organized crime. Where before they had
been at a disadvantage due to the normal rules of
evidence and procedure, RICO changed everything. Not
only did it allow them to steamroller the Mafia and put
the big bosses behind bars. It also gave them a powerful
weapon to use against ordinary business owners, if the
feds chose to target them. In fact it gave them the power
to prosecute pretty well anybody they didn't like.

Very few people seem to notice this. Maybe it's because
they themselves haven't been victims of an unjust RICO
prosecution. Judges, lawmakers and the media keep

cheering on federal prosecutors as they blithely overturn the due process guarantees of the constitution. And as one commentator has written, "overturn" is not to strong a word when we realize that people charged in a RICO case are treated as guilty unless they can be proven innocent.

But wait a minute! Isn't that contrary to the Fourth Amendment? Aren't criminal defendants supposed to be considered innocent until proven guilty? Not under RICO. Wiping its behind with the Fourth Amendment, RICO allows government to seize entire businesses, all assets including bank accounts, if they can be made to appear connected to an indicted defendant - without any proof of guilt!

It's like *Saturday Night Live*. RICO lets the government be prosecutor, judge and jury all at once, in the same case.

In our case the feds took full advantage of the RICO provisions that, when it came to proof, allowed their pair of deuces to trump our royal flush. The first move they made after presenting that mixture of truth, half-truth and lies to get the grand jury to indict us, was one that stuffed a couple more extra aces up their sleeve. They entered a pre-trial *Motion In Limine*, literally a motion "at the threshold." Like the *Santiago Proffer* of the grand jury proceeding, the *motion in limine* asks the court to admit the testimony of three people nobody would ever accuse of fanatical devotion to the truth, Nick LoBue, Ralph Galderio and Don Prisco, *as if it were established fact.*

Starting with the heading, **Notice of Intention to Introduce Evidence Concerning Receipt of Bribe from Rod Costello**, the document drones on with one unsubstantiated fiction after another.

"Sometime (after July 1989) ... Mayor Chuck Panici informed LoBue that Costello would have to come up with a payoff."

Really? Who says such a thing and where's the proof? Oh, look! It turns out this exciting information came from none other than Nick LoBue. Isn't he the admitted lifelong liar? Well, LoBue is a government witness, so whatever he says must be reliable. -- Hmm!

The motion drones on and on in the same preposterous vein. To a reader with sharp eyes and an open mind the true situation soon becomes clear. Such a reader exclaims, "Holy sh.. , or rather, My word! This guy LoBue has been shaking down everybody in sight ever since he took office, and now he's wriggling off the hook by fingering the mayor and two other commissioners!"

Go to the head of the class, sharp-eyed reader! But just wait. On page 19 of their motion the prosecutors utter their biggest whopper of all - a lie originating like all the others from Nick LoBue's fevered imagination.

"On April 25, 1991, [Water Commissioner Louise] Marshall was interviewed by Special Agent Neal O'Malley. " *(Why are so many of these government guys "special?")* This final piece of fiction goes on to say, "Marshall confessed *(sic!)* to O'Malley that she had strongly suspected that Panici, Gliottoni and LoBue were taking money on the pipeline contract and that she twice approached LoBue and asked to 'be part of it.' LoBue denied any money was being distributed. -- After asking Panici to cut her in as well, Marshall approached [Mob boss Albert "Caesar"] Tocco for help. Marshall explained that she went to Tocco because 'she always heard the Mafia was fair and that they would not want her to be unhappy.' However Tocco did not in fact offer Marshall any assistance."

Let's take this prosecution whopper apart piece by piece. First the purported interview between Louise Marshall and "Special Agent" O'Malley. Did it really take place? Other than the unsubstantiated (but "special") word of O'Malley himself, no proof was ever offered to the court or anyone else to confirm that O'Malley ever had this mysterious interview with Louise Marshall. All of the FBI's interviews with "persons of interest" are taken down as Form 302 documents, not nearly as credible as the audio recordings which nowadays are standard procedure in Britain, Canada and other Common Law countries, but better than nothing at all. O'Malley was able to produce nothing at all. FBI agents are known to lie like sidewalks on occasion, but even "special" ones have to draw the line at forging a fake confession.

The story is ridiculous for that reason alone! But now, here's the second glaring untruth in O'Malley's "Special

Agent" story. Albert Tocco was a notorious Mob figure in Chicago Heights, but he had no hand in our water pipeline project, that long and arduous process that was such a proud achievement of our administration. Tocco had a totally different kind of relationship with the City of Chicago Heights. He was the indirect owner of a waste disposal company that served the city. But he had nothing to offer a bribe seeker - not even Nick LoBue - in connection with the water pipeline.

And just how was Louise Marshall supposed to have "approached" the scary-looking Mob boss whose picture you see in this chapter? Did she phone for an appointment? Do Mob bosses see people that way? Do they keep office hours? They're typically found in the company of large, tough well-armed bodyguards. You don't just walk in and have a chat. Somebody else sees you come and go. And Louise's purported "confession?" Pure unmixed imagination. The only corroboration that was ever offered came during the trial itself from Assistant US Attorney Chris Gair. Gair claimed that he had been present during the imaginary "confession" but he wouldn't say it under oath. He was probably the co-author of a faked confession but didn't want to be caught committing perjury.

In making that claim but refusing to testify under oath, Chris Gair violated the Advocate Witness Rule. That rule says a lawyer who wishes to enter his or her own testimony in evidence must be sworn in as a witness like anyone else. The rule excuses the advocate witness from having to testify under oath unless the testimony is "essential." And if testimony proving the guilt or innocence of a 70-year-old African American woman, and her two co-defendants, isn't "essential" what the hell is?

But on this point, as on a number of others, trial judge James B. Zagel leaped to Chris Gair's aid. In a similar way, and probably for similar reasons, Judge Zagel bent over backwards throughout our trial in his efforts not to piss off the prosecutors. I'll say more about that later. Zagel's bias becomes pathetically obvious when we take a statistical sample of his rulings in favor of the prosecution and contrast them with his far less frequent rulings in favor of the defense. 81% of his rulings supported the prosecution. 19% favored the defense.

But guess what? None of this matters a tinker's damn! These were RICO charges, remember? When it came right down to it, the prosecutors didn't have to prove any of their lies and half-truths. All they needed to do was show that there might have been a conspiracy to commit two or more criminal acts. And the RICO definition of a conspiracy is "two or more people."

So the motion *in limine* was granted and the trial proceeded according to the prosecutors' plan. And as it progressed I came to realize that my innocence wasn't going to be nearly as easy to prove as I had believed. There are some fabulously skillful defense attorneys in Chicago. One of the very best, Allan A. Ackerman, was later to argue my appeal. I wish I had engaged him to conduct my defense!

Mr. Ackerman has said, "The role of counsel as constitutionally demanded is to do what is necessary to represent a client in preparation for trial. Younger lawyers don't have the wealth of experience and federal knowledge (required) to get to the points of law to be presented on behalf of accused in advance of trial".

How might Allan Ackerman have handled that outrageous motion *in limine*? We can only wonder.

Chapter Ten
Courtroom Drama, Or Theater Of The Absurd?

One way or another, we all know something about the *Theater of the Absurd*.

It was a French critic named *Martin Esslin* who first used the term in 1960, but the thing itself existed long before that. It describes the kind of drama that *Samuel Beckett, Eugene Ionesco, Harold Pinter and Edward Albee* have been producing for more than half a century. But this kind of tragic comedy, or *tragicomedy*, goes back a lot further. You can find it in Shakespeare back in the 16th century and even earlier in Dante Alighieri's *Divina Commedia (Divine Comedy)*,in the 14th century, especially the first part titled *Inferno (Hell)*.

Here's a quick definition for you. In Samuel Beckett's play *Endgame* a character named Nell says, "Nothing is funnier than unhappiness ... it's the most comical thing in the world."

I guess I can relate to that. And so would my dear friends John Gliottoni and Louise Marshall if they were

148

still alive to enjoy the joke. But as I've already told you and will tell you again, I don't buy the idea that life is meaningless. My life is what I make it and yours will be too, if you develop the right attitude. This book has an appendix that offers you some help in that regard.

Still, the Theater of the Absurd portrays life as a random process and humans as marionettes controlled by an offstage puppeteer named Fate. If we change "life" to "justice" and "Fate" to "US Prosecutor's Office" we get a pretty good outline of the trial that sent me and my two colleagues to prison.

I have attempted several times to write an account of that trial, in a way that exposes and underlines the tricks and techniques that persuaded twelve jurors to convict us without once being shown any credible evidence. It's impossible to do that. There were thirteen counts against us, all stemming from that wonderful RICO Act we looked at in the chapter before this. The indictment alone is so lengthy and convoluted that it makes your head ache. The testimony takes so many twists and turns that you need to trace your way through it with a ball of twine like Theseus, the guy in the Labyrinth hunting the

Minotaur.

And eventually I realized why that is. The trial was designed and planned that way. It was *meant* to be so complicated that it seems incomprehensible. The very complexity of the trial is the key to how they got the verdict they wanted. Once you become aware of this, you know where to look and how to describe it. You have to follow the prosecutors' game plan from start to finish. Skip over all the confusing *details* and see the *pattern*.

It's impossible to tell whether any of the prosecutors sincerely believed what Nick LoBue told them. If you ask them they can only say, "Of course. We saw our duty to do justice and we did it."

Why? Because if they realized that LoBue was lying to them, but proceeded in spite of that knowledge, they themselves would be in hot water. That would be *suborning perjury*, an all too common form of prosecutorial misconduct which is also a criminal offense. Time and again the appeal courts discover that prosecutors have committed the offense of suborning perjury. Their favorite way of letting offending prosecutors off the hook is the ***doctrine of harmless error***. "Harmless" my foot! Mind you, in lawyers' jargon "harmless" has a special meaning, equivalent to "not done on purpose in a way that would be actionable."

But it goes deeper. The rules of procedure place an additional burden of truthfulness on lawyers. It applies primarily to defense attorneys but it covers prosecutors too. Remember that American Bar Association rule that I quoted earlier.

If the lawyer knows, from the client's clearly stated intention, that the client will testify falsely, and the lawyer cannot effectively withdraw from the representation, the lawyer must either limit the examination of the client to subjects on which the lawyer believes the client will testify truthfully; or, if there are none, not permit the client to testify; or, if this is not feasible, disclose the client's intention to testify falsely to the tribunal.

My impression, based on what they actually said and did, is that the prosecutors may have known full well that Nick LoBue was telling them fantastic lies in the hope of not spending the rest of his life in jail. But they could proceed *as if* they thought LoBue's stories were gospel truth. After all, they were experienced masters of RICO prosecution. RICO gave them summary powers the old Soviet KGB would have envied. They didn't need to prove us guilty of any crime in particular. Those are what the RICO Act calls the "predicate" crimes. All they had to do was get a jury to believe there was a *conspiracy* to commit crimes. Under RICO it's the conspiracy that counts, not the real or imagined crimes. So that was the mainspring of their case. But as we've already seen, they had a major problem - no evidence.

The FBI spent a lot of time and money trying to build a *prime facie* case against me. They watched me, took pictures of me, tapped my phone calls, subpoenaed my bank records - every trick they knew that might have given them proof that I was somehow receiving and concealing large amounts of cash. Well, come on! They knew as well as you and I do that it's impossible to conceal large amounts of money. Thousands have tried to do it. All have been caught. Sooner or later you have to get all that money into the lawful banking system, the process known as "money laundering" - turning illegal cash into a legal account balance. And that's where the FBI, the IRS, the FDA or any sharp-eyed auditor can spot what you're doing.

With me they found zero. There was nothing to find. My bank accounts, my tax returns and my other financial affairs, both personal and corporate, checked out perfectly. When it came to hard evidence they found Chuck Panici clean as a whistle.

With Nick LoBue it was a very different story. Him they had nailed without even breathing hard. You may recall that LoBue and Donald Prisco were co-owners of a currency exchange. They were also enthusiastic gamblers. Not successful but enthusiastic. I knew LoBue of course because we worked together in the city administration. I had known Don Prisco for years too because we were both in municipal politics. But we were hardly the bosom buddies the reporters portrayed when they wrote about us.

LoBue and Prisco were not only partners in business; they became partners in disaster too when in 1990 they were indicted on 16 RICO counts of racketeering, conspiracy and tax fraud. Newspaper reports described them as "business partners, owning a currency exchange in Chicago Heights that was allegedly used to funnel payoffs to themselves in the form of checks made out to fictitious people and cashed at the exchange."

That's pretty well it in a nutshell. There was plenty of evidence to convict both LoBue and Prisco. LoBue in particular left a well marked trail to document his wrongdoing. The FBI's forensic accountants had no trouble figuring out where he had been and what he had done.

But what of different picture we see one year later! LoBue's no longer headed for a lifetime in prison. Nor is Don Prisco, who is already in jail but has been offered a deal that will radically shorten his prison term. The big difference is that LoBue has decided to "cooperate" with the government. All of a sudden, he remembers events never before mentioned either in his indictment or his prior testimony. In return for this sudden flood of new memories, which implicate Panici, Gliottoni and Marshall in numerous crimes of corruption - hauntingly

154

similar to his own - Nick LoBue is given immunity from prosecution. All he has to do, together with the three other prosecution witnesses, is shift the blame from himself onto the shoulders of Panici, Gliottoni and Marshall.

Chapter Eleven
Alternate Realities

The transcript of our trial is a long, bloated document. You can read on my website the parts of it that matter. You can also get to it by way of my Facebook page.

But here's the thing. Long and complex as it is, the transcript becomes plain and simple once we look at it with our x-ray vision. When we look right through the smoke and mirrors and see the simple bone structure of the trial, we see that two versions of the facts are presented side by side. Alternate realities.

The prosecution version, as I have said over and over, rests entirely on the untruthful testimony of Nick LoBue. I don't balk at saying "untruthful" because it's so easy to see that LoBue is an unreliable witness. Not only are his stories full of gaps and inconsistencies. They are also uncorroborated. No credible evidence supports LoBue's testimony. There was no *disinterested* witness, no one with *nothing to gain or lose* in the trial, who confirmed anything that LoBue said.

The prosecutors did call witnesses who supposedly substantiated what LoBue was saying. But those three witnesses - Ralph Galderio, Donald Prisco and Rodney

156

Costello - were no more reliable than LoBue. Why?
Because in return for leniency, all were coerced and
bribed to say what the prosecutors told them to say on
the witness stand. There were other witnesses who
confirmed that the crimes in question had really been
committed. But none of those witnesses implicated
Charles Panici, John Gliottoni or Louise Marshall. The
reality is that their testimony pointed the finger of guilt
at the prosecution witnesses! All of the credible
evidence points to LoBue, Prisco, Galderio and
Costello!

To make this really clear, let's go step by step through
the prosecution's RICO case, based on the lies and half-
truths of Nick LoBue, and compare it with the actual
facts, based on history as recalled by me and others.
And as we compare the two stories, remember that in a
trial, a half truth is the same as an outright lie.

And before we begin, here is something that reveals a lot
about Chris Gair, the lead prosecutor. During our trial
Gair praised Nick LoBue for showing "repentance" and
agreeing to testify on behalf of the government in return
for the promise of immunity from prosecution. But a
few years later when he became a defense attorney

specializing in white collar crime, Gair had quite a different attitude about witnesses who have been granted immunity.

"John Henry has been granted immunity in exchange for his testimony," Gair told the court while defending former Chicago Treasurer Miriam Santos. "Therefore he cannot be trusted. Nor can several others (former employees of the defendant) who will take the stand." Who would know better than Chris Gair how little we can rely on a witness who has been granted immunity? He has been there. He has done it himself. He knows how it is done. I think philosophers have a term for the way lawyers can switch sides without batting an eye. They call it "moral relativism."

Nevertheless if you are accused of a white collar crime you could do worse than to hire Chris Gair to defend you! He's wise to all the federal prosecutors' favorite tricks.

The Alternate Realities

Prosecutors' Version: *The three defendants conspired with LoBue and others to operate the city of Chicago Heights through a pattern of extortion, bribery and* *official misconduct.*

Reality: Nick LoBue, acting alone and for his own benefit both before and after becoming finance commissioner of Chicago Heights, solicited and extorted bribes and kickbacks from contractors who did business with the city, conspiring from time to time with Mob boss Albert "Caesar" Tocco. He sometimes included Prisco, Galderio or Costello in his schemes.

Prosecutors: *The defendants, along with Nick LoBue and Donald Prisco, solicited, demanded and agree to accept bribe payments from companies and individuals who did business with the City of Chicago Heights and actually received more than $600,000 in such payoffs.*

Reality: Nick LoBue and Donald Prisco, together with Ralph Galderio, Rodney Costello, Albert Tocco and others, solicited and accepted bribe payments whose amount cannot possibly be determined. No evidence substantiates a figure like $600,000.

Prosecutors: *The defendants used "bagmen," of whom LoBue was one, to collect their bribery payments.*

Reality: There were no "bagmen." LoBue, Prisco and Galderio personally received the bribe payments and pocketed the money themselves.

Prosecutors: *From 1977 to 1979, the city ordered shipments of 35,000 pounds of Tri-Lux from Lobue's company, A.A. Arken. However, instead of delivering 35,000 pounds of Tri-Lux, A.A. Arken arranged for the private delivery of only 24,000 pounds of the chemical from Gulf Coast. The city paid Arken for the full 35,000 pounds; Arken paid Gulf Coast for only 24,000 pounds; and LoBue, the owner of Arken, retained the difference and distributed the overpayment between Panici, Gliottoni, himself, Ralph Galderio, and a friend of LoBue's, Mike Costabile.*

Reality: LoBue, the owner of A. A. Arken, retained the difference and distributed the overpayment among himself, Ralph Galderio, and a friend of LoBue's, Mike Costabile. No testimony other than that of LoBue mentions Panici or Gliottoni.

Prosecutors: *In 1979, the city council was considering awarding a contract to provide cable television to the city and, according to city procedure, the council solicited bids from cable television companies. Mayor Panici advised LoBue that he and Gliottoni would be taken care of if they would vote to award the contract to*

160

Telecommunications Inc., a franchise owned by Panici's acquaintance. In a city council vote of May 1981, LoBue and Gliottoni voted as Panici had requested and each of them in turn had their palms greased with a $35,000 payoff.

Reality: In 1979, the city council was indeed awarding a contract to provide cable television to the city and solicited bids from cable television companies. The commissioners voted for Telecommunications Inc. for reasons that anyone can read in the minutes of their meeting. LoBue's underscored words are a fabrication. No evidence exists to indicate the greasing of any palms with ($35,000 x 3 =) $105,000.

Prosecutors: *In 1980, Fitzpatrick Brothers ... bid for the (Chicago Heights) residential trash pickup contract, ... made the payoff and was awarded the three-year contract. It was agreed that the first payment would be made to Don Prisco, the mayor of the neighboring city of South Chicago Heights and a close friend of the defendant Panici. Prisco gave the money to Panici, LoBue and Gliottoni. Altogether, Panici, LoBue, Prisco, and Gliottoni received $20,000 to $30,000 on the residential trash pickup contract.*

Reality: A payoff was in fact made and it was made to LoBue and Prisco, who were gambling partners, deeply in debt. They really needed the money. To cover their debts both men were rumored to have mortgaged their homes. Neither Panici nor Gliottoni knew of any kickback on the trash pick up contract. Before testifying at the trial Prisco sent the handwritten letter *(see photocopy)* in which he mentioned the testimony he was being pressured to give as a condition of his plea bargain with the Feds. [See Ch. 6 on *Prosecutorial Misconduct*]

Prosecutors: *In 1984, the city council voted to increase garbage disposal service from weekly pickups to twice-weekly pickups and doubled the contract payment to Tocco. Accordingly, Tocco's kickback increased from $900 to $1800 per month. To hide the increased payoffs, A.A. Arken, LoBue's company, billed Tocco's garbage disposal company $1800 a month for pest control services at Tocco's company, which were never provided. LoBue deposited Tocco's payoff checks in the Arken company account and then endorsed a check payable to himself for $1800, giving $900 to Mayor Panici.*

Reality: In 1984, responding to community demands,

the city council increased garbage service from weekly to twice-weekly pickups. This doubled the cost of the contract. According to LoBue's account, Tocco's kickback payment thereby doubled from $900 to $1800 per month. To hide the increased payoffs, A.A. Arken, LoBue's company, billed Tocco's garbage disposal company $1800 a month for "pest control" services at Tocco's company, which were never provided. LoBue deposited Tocco's "pest control" checks in the Arken company account and then endorsed a check for $1800 payable to himself.

Prosecutors: *In 1980, Charles Fitzpatrick and (Marty) Wondaal decided to form a corporation named Fitz-Mar, in hopes of securing a contract with Chicago Heights to operate the city's landfill. Fitzpatrick and Wondaal met with Don Prisco and negotiated the amount of payment required to secure the contract. Prisco informed them that 10 percent of the total revenues would be paid to the city, as legitimate royalties, and 10 percent would be paid to the "boys," in addition to a $20,000 payment up front. ... Accordingly, Wondaal made the payoff with one-ounce gold coins, delivering them to Prisco who in turn gave them to Lobue. Under Panici's instructions, Lobue divided the* *gold coins among Panici, LoBue, Galderio, and Ernie Molyneaux, an individual on the landfill recommendation commission. After the initial payoff, Wondaal made monthly cash payments to LoBue, and they were divided among LoBue, Panici, and Prisco.*

Reality: This is a striking example of the way the prosecutors blended fact and fancy. It is true and was proven that Fitzpatrick and Wondaal made the payments to Don Prisco, and that he in turn gave them to LoBue. The remainder is fiction, uncorroborated by any evidence except the untruthful testimony of the prosecution's four "tame" witnesses. And not even these four are able to agree on the details! It was LoBue, Prisco and Galderio who divided the money.

Prosecutors: *Unrelated to the extortion, concerns arose that the landfill was leaking toxins into the drinking water, and the Environmental Protection Agency ordered the shut down of the landfill operation and brought in a consulting engineer to address the problem. At that time, Mayor Panici told LoBue that the landfill would not reopen unless and until Wondaal brought his payoffs up-to-date. Wondaal paid $30,000 as directed in gold coins to comply with his illegal agreement, with 50*

164

percent going to Mayor Panici, and 25 percent each to Prisco and LoBue.

Reality: No blend of fact and fancy here! It's 100% fantasy. Wondaal never dealt with the mayor. He was dealing with LoBue. The $30,000 in gold coins would make a good story but if such an amount was paid to anyone it was to LoBue. Who would seriously believe the mayor of a city had the authority to overturn a decision of the Environmental Protection Agency?

Prosecutors: *In 1981, a tavern owner in Chicago Heights requested that the hours of his liquor license be extended. Mayor Panici, as head of the liquor commission, was responsible for the control of liquor licenses, including the extension of hours of operation. The tavern owner was instructed by a friend of LoBue, John Graham, to write a letter to Mayor Panici and enclose a $4000 cash payment, which he did; the extension of the operating hours was granted. Graham, LoBue's friend, gave the cash to Ralph Galderio, and the money was split between Panici, Galderio, and LoBue and used to finance a trip to Las Vegas. At trial, city records for the granting of extended hours were produced and reflected only a receipt of $750, the* *standard* fee.

Reality: A tavern owner did request the extension of his liquor license hours. Mayor Panici hesitated to grant the extension because the city was being asked to shorten, not lengthen tavern hours. The extension was eventually granted and the tavern owner paid the standard fee of $750. LoBue and Galderio together cooked up the story of the bribe-financed trip to Las Vegas but they couldn't agree how and when the money changed hands.

Prosecutors: *Robinson Engineering, a local firm headed by Dante DeSantis, joined with a number of contractors to form a joint venture to secure a contract to construct a pipeline to carry water from Lake Michigan to Chicago Heights, rather than drawing it from local wells. Mayor Panici instructed LoBue that there was a need for a kickback from the project, up to 1 or 2 percent of the contract. LoBue met with DeSantis, who spoke with the other contractors and they all agreed to make a combined payment of $100,000 to the city council. LoBue testified that when Louise Marshall became aware of the arrangement, she contacted him and inquired about the payoffs because the project came under the control of the department she supervised, the*

water department. Mayor Panici instructed LoBue that
the payoffs would be split among Panici, LoBue,
Gliottoni, and Marshall. DeSantis delivered the money
in cash to LoBue, who in turn delivered $25,000 to each
of the commissioners at their homes, as well as to
Marshall at her home.

Reality: This one is full of "traverses," a lawyer's word
for conflicting versions of the facts! Robinson
Engineering did form a joint venture. Dante Desantis
did "funnel" (his exact word) $100,000 to Nick LoBue.
Not all of the money was "delivered in cash." Part of it
was a check in the amount of $45,002.48. LoBue was
careless enough to "squeal" on himself by clearing that
sizeable check through his own currency exchange!
LoBue delivered no cash to anyone but himself.
Whatever form the bribe took, he put the money in his
pocket. His underlined comments are entirely
untruthful.

Especially vicious is LoBue's lie about Louise Marshall.
I've mentioned before that Louise Marshall was
everything that's right about local government. When a
slimy little sleazeball crook like Nick LoBue shifts the
blame for his own crimes onto a God fearing 71-year-

year-old African American woman, I can't help turning red and grinding my teeth!

Equally outrageous was the claim of FBI Case Agent O'Malley that Louise had "confessed" to him the alleged involvement in LoBue's water pipeline kickback. She had made no such confession. The accusation was an ugly lie. But on the witness stand O'Malley stuck to his lie, or mistake, whichever it was. He couldn't produce any written record of the imaginary "confession," much less an audio recording. The probability is that Chris Gair, while questioning Louise Marshall, expected her to crumble in the face of O'Malley's untruthful testimony.

What happened was the very opposite. Louise resolutely denied everything O'Malley said. That left Prosecutor Gair, who claimed to have been present during two of O'Malley's interviews, in an awkward spot. He made it out that he could personally vouch for O'Malley's story. No audio recording, not even a written report - but Gair was willing to testify from memory! The idea that an FBI agent might - gasp! - knowingly give false testimony made Gair all but faint in dismay.

The Advocate Witness Rule

And here we come to the notorious **Advocate Witness Rule**. That rule says that if an attorney wants to testify, he has to be sworn in like any other witness. But Chris Gair desperately wanted *not* to testify under oath. Afraid of being caught giving perjured testimony? I don't say it but you're free to consider the possibility.

Gair was right in fearing that Louise Marshall's evidence could destroy his entire case. All through the trial Gair, McLellan and Foreman had been gaming the judge and jury with the notion that if one government witness uttered a lie and three other government witnesses told the same or similar lies, their combined lies added up to "overwhelming evidence." That was how they were hoping to work around the fact that they didn't have any physical evidence at all! In order to win they had to prove that there had been a *conspiracy* which involved *racketeering*. The linchpin of that argument was the story of Louise Marshall's supposed meeting with Albert Tocco. If they couldn't prove that, the remainder of their case would hang limp and empty, as in fact it was.

And of course they couldn't prove it! The story is simply ridiculous. Albert Tocco refused to answer any questions whatsoever. He certainly didn't tell of a meeting with any elderly black lady to discuss payoffs. FBI Special Agent O'Malley is no help either. As far as proof is concerned, O'Malley's story could as easily have been a dream or a hallucination.

The lawyer who argued my appeal put his finger on this pivotal weakness of the government's case. To a sharp-eyed defense attorney like Allan Ackerman the government's case had a gaping hole. His list of flaws observed that the prosecutors had *"... no physical evidence against Panici, and no produced or credible evidence of any unaccounted for assets or spending;"* All the prosecutors were able to produce, Ackerman wrote, were *"... tainted and highly biased key prosecution witnesses;"* who all gave *"... knowingly perjured and coached testimony, directly contradicting in many key material elements the government's own proffers or court filings. "*

So was FBI Special Agent Neal O'Malley lying or was he just mistaken? Let's think about it. The standard practice of the FBI when interviewing a person of interest was to write a report, the well known Form FD-302. As we have noted, that's far from being the best way to document an interview - the best way is to make

170

an audio recording of it - but the FBI doesn't do that. In this case O'Malley certainly had no audio recording. He didn't have a 302 either. He didn't even have any handwritten notes that he would surely have made while interviewing Louise Marshall.

Small wonder that prosecutor Chris Gair got flustered as a wet hen when Louise Marshall totally contradicted Agent O'Malley! He could see how fishy O'Malley's story might look to the jury. There was absolutely no proof! Would an FBI special agent tell a lie? Don't make me laugh! Can you spell "Whitey Bulger?" Did you see "The Departed?"

As it happens there is case law on the matter of perjured government testimony. In the noted case *US v. Boyd* the following was established.

The government must correct false testimony of a government witness, whether the testimony is elicited upon direct examination by the prosecutor, or whether elicited on cross examination by defense counsel. In other words, to the extent the government allows such testimony to go uncorrected, perjured testimony will be considered a part of the government's case, even if elicited by defense counsel on cross examination. To be sure, where the defense counsel is unaware that he has elicited perjured testimony because the government has not corrected the statement it knew to be false, then in a very real sense the government is the party using the false testimony.

The transcript shows that Gair was well aware of this. He all but grovels before the bench as he pleads not to be made to testify under oath. "My recollection is the same as Agent O'Malley," he tells the judge. "Why should Mr. Gair be an exception to the Advocate Witness Rule?" Louise's lawyer asks. In the end Judge James B. Zagel let Gair off the hook. Demonstrating once again his not-always-quiet enthusiasm for the government's case, he excused Gair from having to testify on the grounds that "the defense had not called Mr. Gair as a witness."

This wasn't just a lawyers' squabble over procedure. It was a matter of guilt or innocence for a 70 year old woman, accused on the strength of no evidence at all beyond the perjured word of a pathological liar and the unsupported memory of an FBI agent with no written evidence, not even handwritten notes. With that ruling Judge Zagel showed either that he was working hand in glove with the prosecutors or that he was himself

172

threatened with prosecution if he failed to help the government's case. As you saw in Chapter Six, threatening judges with prosecution is a fairly common form of prosecutor misconduct.

This is no idle notion. in the coming chapter I will show you proof that Judge James B. Zagel rarely failed to favor the prosecution during his entire conduct of the trial. In the jargon of the appellate courts he "abused his discretion" time and time again. I'll give you just one example here and now. A fair and competent judge would have made sure the jury understood that the four key prosecution witnesses: LoBue, Prisco, Galderio and Costello, all had been richly rewarded for saying what the prosecutors told them to say. They weren't even charged with the RICO crimes they had already confessed to.

Chief Judge Richard Posner of the Seventh District Circuit Court put his finger on this very question of untruthful prosecution witnesses in the case I just mentioned, *US v. Boyd*.

Do you throw a birthday party for a man who you think deserves to spend his life behind bars? Might not a reasonable jury have concluded, had they known all the facts, that the prosecution team must have had desperate doubts about the testimonial reliability of these witnesses to have lavished such extraordinary personal attentions upon them? In short, might not the prosecution's case have collapsed entirely had the truth come out about the behavior and the treatment of these witnesses?

As I am about to show you, more experienced attorneys would have conducted a more successful defense. Not even the a biased (or intimidated) judge could have kept the jury from seeing the truth if a defense attorney of Allan Ackerman's caliber had handled our case. The problem with inexperienced lawyers is that they don't know they're inexperienced. And we didn't either.

Chapter Twelve
Before the Law Some Are More Equal Than Others

You may have noticed that throughout this book I have been slipping in little bits of advice from time to time. Here's another one. If you are ever charged with a crime, be sure to hire the best possible lawyer to defend you. Never mind how much he or she may cost you. The important thing is that your lawyer be the most skilled, experienced and famous you can find.

I'll tell you why. First of all, a famous attorney usually does the best job. That's the reason for the fame. His or her very reputation causes both judge and jury to listen with a special kind of respect. There was nothing special about the lawyers who argued our case that would have made an impression on either Judge James B. Zagel or the twelve members of the jury. But if a Clarence Darrow, a Melvin Belli or a Johnnie Cochran had argued our case, we would have heard that respectful silence that only famous lawyers can generate whenever they rise to speak.

You think I'm kidding? Then tell me why O.J. Simpson

was acquitted despite the fact that he was the only person who could have killed his wife, while I and my two colleagues were convicted without any physical evidence or credible testimony. It makes a very, very important difference who your lawyer is. I know, it's water under the bridge from where we stand now, but that George Santayana quotation is right. If we don't learn from our experience we'll have to go through it all over again.

I'm not saying that the lawyers who represented us were not good at their job. It's just that all but one were beyond their depth in the murky waters of a RICO case. The exception was John Gliottoni's counsel, Anthony Onesto, who had a good track record and a good reputation. Meanwhile their adversaries, the prosecutors, were people well known to the judge and also to many members of the jury, simply because they were so often both in court and in the news. They weren't so much <u>better</u> lawyers. They were <u>better</u> <u>prepared</u> lawyers.

And that is one place where the rubber meets the road, as the saying goes. Looking back on my own experience, I can see the qualities in a trial lawyer that make him or her stand out from the rest of the crowd. Not only do the really good lawyers possess ample knowledge and experience. They also have an exceptional <u>command of language</u>, even though they may not always come out with rhyming slogans like Johnnie Cochran's "If it doesn't fit you must acquit!" They are also meticulously <u>prepared</u>, as a rule, for the task they face. I believe a first rate lawyer might have succeeded in getting the court to <u>sever</u> our three trials - hear them individually - on the grounds that John Gliottoni and I stood no chance of getting a fair trial so long as our fate depended on that of Louise Marshall. The indictment against her depended on proving that she had connections with organized crime, and if such a connection were proved then Gliottoni and Panici would be guilty by association, not by proof.

That was one reason why, late in the trial, I engaged Ackerman as senior counsel in my defense. Unfortunately I brought him in far too late to undo the damage my defense had already suffered. Ackerman was confident that if he had been able to conduct a skillful cross-examination of Nick LoBue - "impeach" his credibility in lawyers' jargon - he could not only have exposed LoBue's untruthful testimony but also shown the jury the underlying reason for LoBue's bias and slipperiness on the stand - the plea bargain that saved him from many years of imprisonment.

Allan A. Ackerman, gunslinger defender

Which brings to mind another bit of advice I want a pass on to you. If you are ever charged with a serious crime, do your very best to get a "bench" trial before a single judge, rather than a jury trial. It's true that in order to get this kind of trial you need the consent of both the prosecution and the court. But on the other hand it's a request that should not be "unreasonably refused." There are two reasons to seek trial by judge alone. First the judge has the duty of bringing to bear all of his or her knowledge and experience on any legal matter. He or she is expected not to miss anything. The jury has no such obligation. They're just ordinary people. No one

178

expects them to be particularly smart or observant or even reasonable. The second reason is that it's much less difficult to win an appeal from a judge's verdict than from the verdict of a jury. The reason, once again, is that judges are expected not to "misdirect themselves" when reaching a verdict based on the evidence they have heard. The senior judges of an appeal court are much more willing to overturn the verdict of a judge than that of a jury.

There's something else that Allan Ackerman could have done for me, if I had hired him early enough. The pre-trial procedure known as *Discovery and Inspection* gives both sides the right to examine the people who will testify for the other side and to get copies of any documents the other side intends to enter as evidence.

Upon a defendant's request, the government must permit the defendant to inspect and to copy or photograph books, papers, documents, data, photographs, tangible objects, buildings or places, or copies or portions of any of these items, if the item is within the government's possession, custody, or control and:

(i) the item is material to preparing the defense;

(ii) the government intends to use the item in its case-in-chief at trial; or

(iii) the item was obtained from or belongs to the defendant.

Our legal team did request those items but the prosecutors did not fully comply. They kept from us a few of their tastier items. And the judge let them get away with it. The most outrageous example of this was the fantasy "confession" of Louise Marshall. At every court session of the prosecutors trundled in the huge stacks of documents, mainly for the purpose of impressing the jury with the amount of evidence they had. But when it came to documenting Louise Marshall's supposed confession to FBI Special Agent O'Malley there was not one single document. Certainly no statement signed by the defendant, which is how the FBI always handles a confession. Why no proof on so vital a point? And why did Judge Zagel choose that moment to doze off on the job?

If a party fails to comply with this rule, the court may:

(A) order that party to permit the discovery or inspection; specify its time, place, and manner; and prescribe other just terms and conditions;

(B) grant a continuance;

(C) prohibit that party from introducing the undisclosed evidence; or

(D) enter any other order that is just under the circumstances.

Did Judge James B. Zagel order any of these remedies and corrections? Nope! Judge Zagel was in the prosecutors' pocket from the very beginning. So here is one more crucial point where a top-gun lawyer like Allan Ackerman might have made all the difference. He made it clear to me, when I finally did engage him to represent me at the very end of our trial, that we had missed a number of opportunities that might have won us acquittal, or at least a retrial on appeal.

At several points during the trial the basic "traverses" or "clashes" between prosecution testimony and that of the defense became very clear. These were the "alternate realities" we talked about earlier. Those were the points at which the government witnesses could have been *impeached*. They could have been cross examined in ways that clearly showed how the prosecutors had coached them to lie on the witness stand. On many points the prosecution witnesses did not agree. Nor did their stories always match the documents the prosecutors had filed. All of this would have put Judge Zagel on the spot. He could have been made either to exclude the obvious lies of the government witnesses or to commit the errors in law that give an appeal court no choice but to overturn a conviction or order a new trial.

Again, this is "water under the bridge" as the saying goes. And I mention these points for your benefit, not mine. If you are ever charged with a serious crime here is an important list for you to follow.

1 Engage the most capable and well-known defense attorney you can find, regardless of cost. Ineffective

counsel will cost you a lot more than the most expensive defense lawyer. A well known lawyer helps you not only in the courtroom but also in the media.

2 Discuss every aspect of your case, long and often, with your legal team. Make sure nothing gets overlooked. If our defense team had been vigilant, we could have shot down the prosecutors' fake story of Louise Marshall meeting with Albert Tocco and turned that lie to our advantage.

3 Get your side of the story of out into the media at every opportunity. The media, and especially television, very often determine the outcome of the trial. Sure, the judge tells the jurors not to discuss the case and not to read about it, but how many jury members really do avoid the newspaper and TV reports?

Chapter Thirteen
More Free Advice - Media Management

In this part of my story I am offering you quite a bit of important advice arising out of my own experience. And please understand, I'm not just talking off the top of my head. I have had a lot of time to think about these things. And I got good advice too from some of the people I met during my eight year stay in Duluth.

But in this chapter I will discuss an aspect of our trial and conviction that I didn't seriously think about during or after the event. The mass media: television, radio and the press, were a big factor in the outcome of our trial. Looking over the newspaper clippings and remembering the TV reports, I'm beginning to think the media had more influence on the jury's verdict than the lawyers.

There's a major flaw in our legal system. During the course of a trial the judge reminds the jury at the end of each day's session that they are not to discuss the case they are hearing with anyone else or with each other. How many jury members actually comply? If you're called as a juror and you go home for dinner after each day's court session, are you going to make your family turn off the TV whenever there's a report about your trial? Are you going to turn away your gaze when you open the front door to find a newspaper with the headline about the trial you are hearing?

I don't think so. Maybe it was possible in the 18th century for a jury member to isolate himself - in the 1700s he would always have been a male - from all discussion or mention of a trial. But in today's world, with TV, radio, the daily press and the Internet all blaring headlines about each and every public event, how can a juror avoid hearing what others say about a legal case? No way!

You'll notice that I list the media in a certain order: TV, radio and the daily press. The reason is that television has by far the greatest influence on public opinion. Radio is the second most influential. And from the two electronic media there is quite a gap down to the daily press, which is nowhere near as influential as it used to be. But even though there is "nothing so out of date as yesterday's newspaper," headlines and clippings do provide a permanent record of what has been said. The fourth and very new factor is the Internet. A huge and growing number of people rely on the World Wide Web for local, national and global news. On the Internet they can get video, audio and text reports of what's going on in the world. They also get a far *wider range of viewpoints* than the daily mainstream media provide.

So it is that ownership of a newspaper or a TV station is no longer the big-money monopoly that it used to be. The Internet with its "blogosphere" gives everybody a platform for whatever they want to say. And that is why I can now present my account through my own website, my own social media page and this electronic book even more effectively than the Chicago Tribune and the Chicago Sun times were able to do in the early 1990s.

In those days it was a different world. We were led to believe that the news media were in the business of finding the facts and presenting them "in a balanced manner" to the public. That's what they always told us. The truth was different. For the owners of the mass media news and public affairs are a *commodity*, a product they can distribute to their viewers, listeners or readers in such large numbers that advertisers will pay

186

them big money to reach the same audience.

There's nothing wrong with that, so long as everyone understands what's going on. The problems begin when editors start looking for sensational headlines purely for the sake of attracting a larger audience. We've all seen the old movies were the newspaper editor tells his reporters to "get me a story that will blow this town wide open!" Under those conditions does the story have to be true in every detail? Does it have to be balanced? Not necessarily. The top priority is to get the headlines and pull in the readers. That in turn brings in the advertising bucks that keep the doors open and the paychecks coming.

When editorial decisions are made solely for the sake of capturing readers, with no regard whatsoever for facts, we have the notorious Tabloid Press. Not just the National Enquirer on the rack at your supermarket checkout shrieking headlines like, "Elvis and Diana love nest in Milwaukee parking lot!" Many "respectable" daily newspapers too are sinking into the brand of journalism that places headline grabbing sensation ahead of factual truth. Sadly that was the situation at the

Chicago Tribune, Sun Times and lesser periodicals in
1992 when our trial was in the news.

Check out these reports.

Chicago Heights Bagman Details Web Of Corruption
*An admittedly corrupt former Chicago Heights city
commissioner detailing rampant corruption in the south
suburb Tuesday alleged that Robert Grossi, supervisor
of Bloom Township, took bribes from him.*
*Nick LoBue, testifying in federal court at the trial of
former Chicago Heights Mayor Charles Panici,
recounted dozens of payoffs and hundreds of thousands
of dollars in bribes he said he passed along to Panici
and others as the "bagman" for a corrupt circle of
politicians.*
*With Panici's support, LoBue said he then ran for City
Council, winning election in 1979. In a sham, LoBue
withdrew as the chemical supplier for conflict-of-interest
reasons, but arranged with owners of Gulf Coast
Laboratories to continue the payoffs to himself, Panici
and the others.*

That's Matt O'Connor writing in the Chicago Tribune in

February 1993. What he's doing is repeating word for word what the prosecutors told Nick LoBue to say on the witness stand. Expressions like "rampant corruption" are straight out of the prosecutor's opening statement. Did the Tribune publish an equally sensational account of LoBue's cross-examination challenging everything he said? Are you kidding?

Chicago Hts. Defendant Denies Taking Kickbacks

Former Chicago Heights City Councilwoman Louise Marshall denied Tuesday that she ever accepted kickbacks, made incriminating statements to FBI agents or visited convicted mobster Albert Tocco.
Testifying in her own defense, Marshall insisted she never accepted kickbacks on a city water pipeline contract or for city plumbing work during her 16 years as a Council member.
Former Chicago Heights City Council member Nick LoBue and city plumbing contractor Gene Wuest have testified they funneled kickbacks to Marshall.

This one is from the Chicago Sun times and like so many it's wrong and misleading. Wuest told of funneling money to LoBue. LoBue said he shared it with

Louise Marshall. Tribune reporters simply repeated whatever the prosecutors said as if it were accomplished fact. The Sun Times was no better at telling both sides of the story. Both papers were focused more on whipping up the readers than finding out the facts.

These newspaper reports, and television reports that were usually even more sensational than the papers, can't have failed to influence the jury in its eventual decision to convict. Not only did the jury not isolate itself from the media reports in compliance with the judge's pious instructions; it looks to me like they allowed the media to do their thinking for them.

So here is my next piece of advice for you in the event that you are ever charged with a serious crime. Make sure that your version of the story gets out into the media. Don't allow the prosecution to hog the headlines. You'll probably need to hire professional media relations practitioners. You should do so without hesitation, no matter what the cost. A public trial - sad to say - is very similar to an election. The outcome is decided mainly in the media. You don't just want headlines. You want headlines with your positive spin.

190

Your media management checklist:

1 Engage professionals to manage your media relations.

2 Make sure that your version of the story is heard first and loudest. If a negative story comes out, be sure to counter with your own rebuttal.

3 Expect the worst behaviour and lowest motives in the reporters, photographers and cameramen who cover your trial. You won't be disappointed. Your media management professionals will know how to throw them the kind of garbage they love.

I realize these remarks and may sound cynical. They're based on my own experience. But please remember, I'm talking about the "big time" media, the TV stations and newspapers in the big urban markets who are always scrambling for the top buck. With the little local stations and local papers it's totally different. These are people who work for low wages because they love the work they do. They really do have the sincere interest in the truth. They want to find out what actually happened.

They enjoy publishing good news as well as bad.

I have more respect for these local media; they've usually treated me fairly. It's the big city media who treat news as a commodity, and who have done me so much harm, that I warn you to handle with care.

Chapter 14
What Have We Learned?

I've said several times in the course of this book that I'm not looking for any favors from the Justice Department. I'm looking to you, the reader, to reach your own verdict on the strength of the facts I have shown you. I don't expect a new trial. I certainly don't expect compensation for the punitive fines -well over $1,000,000 - that I was made to pay because of the injustices of 1993. But I have another motive too.

In the United States of America our system of justice is among the best and fairest in the world. But it's not perfect. No system is. Even though millions of Justice Department people do their best, day after day, to keep the promises our founding fathers made in the Constitution, there will always be a few careerists who are willing to place personal ambition ahead of scruples. Sad to say, Louise Marshall, John Gliottoni and I were victims of that kind of flaw in the system. We fell prey to that "win-at-any-cost" attitude that produces Prosecutorial Misconduct. That is why I have tried to warn you in advance of the hazards you'll face if you are ever in a similar situation.

And for the very same reason I want to make sure that you have the same quality of moral support that I had when I faced my ordeal with the law. I got more effective help from the attitudinal training I have enjoyed throughout my adult life than I did from any external aid or advice. The one single exception was the support of my own family. Their support made all the difference. But if I had been a weaker person, if I had not known for a certainty that I am an honest and moral guy, I could have been destroyed by the monstrous injustice that landed on me in 1993.

But those tough times, horrible as they were, never shook my belief in myself. And as I look back today I can see why more clearly than I could then. It was the superb attitudinal training I had absorbed over the years, principally the program I had personally administered – Adventures In Attitudes. If you're interested I'll tell you all about it.

Meanwhile here in conclusion is a summary of the things I urge you to remember in the event that you are unjustly accused of a criminal offense.

Engage the most capable and reputable defense lawyer you can find.

He or she will cost you a lot of money. Even mediocre lawyers are expensive nowadays! But the losses you can sustain if you're convicted are much greater. Don't just take other people's word for it. Satisfy yourself by finding out how many cases your lawyer has won and how well known those victories are. You don't just need the best lawyer. You need a lawyer everybody *knows* is the best, especially the judge and the jury. You want somebody so good that they make the prosecutors nervous.

You probably don't know enough to find the right lawyer on your own. The people who really know who is best in each field are the lawyers themselves. Ask your local Bar Association about sources that will help you find an attorney with expertise in your particular kind of case. These people specialize. Some do drug cases. Others do personal injury. Still others specialize in DUI cases. They all have track records and the really good ones don't hesitate to make them known. Very often these top people in their field are lecturers or have written book about their field.

And don't assume that you can sit back and relax simply because you have the best available lawyer handling your case. Discuss the case with your defense attorney as often and for as long as necessary to cover each and every point of law and fact that will affect the outcome. Even the greatest experts can overlook an important detail unless someone shows them where to look.

Early in the game a first rate defense attorney will figure out the prosecutors' strategy. And he or she will develop your counterstrategy well before the case goes to trial. Quite often there are pre-trial motions that your attorney can file on your behalf, dealing with constitutional, civil rights or evidence issues than can have a huge effect on the outcome.

If your case is serious and/or sensational, engage reputation management professionals to manage your media relations.

Reputation management is the modern-day buzzword for what we used to call public relations. Looking back on the defeat that we suffered in 1993, I can see that the feds' victory was won first in the mass media and only later in the courtroom. Not only did we lose the battle for public opinion. We weren't even in it. Don't let that happen to you. Hire experienced professionals to protect and advance your reputation.

But in seeking to maintain a good public image make sure you really deserve that image and even then be careful not to overdo it. Former Illinois governor Rod Blagojevich waged his own preemptive war in the media when it was clear he was going to be indicted for corrupt use of his authority to fill the Senate vacancy left by Barack Obama's move to the Whitehouse. He hired Glenn Selig and The Publicity Agency to put his story out before the people. Selig planned an effective campaign but Blagojevich was not an attractive package. The result, putting it kindly, wasn't helpful. Getting fired by Donald Trump on *Celebrity Apprentice* didn't do a lot either for Blago's image as a capable politician.

But that's an extreme case. If you're a reasonably reputable citizen and you're certain you deserve to be acquitted, manage your media issues as carefully as your legal ones. They're part and parcel of a single conflict.

Chapter 15
Summation and Final Argument

I believe it's now time to wrap up my case and conclude our hearing before this Court of Public Opinion. You now have before you my case for the defense. I haven't tried to bury you under a heap of detailed allegations and rebuttals. That's what the prosecution did in 1993. They piled up much testimony and so much paperwork - mostly garbage - that the jury lost sight of the only question that mattered.

Did or did not the prosecutors prove - beyond any reasonable doubt - that Charles Panici, John Gliottoni and Louise Marshall were guilty of the crimes of which they were accused? In the Chapter titled **Alternate Realities** I've summarized for you the prosecutors' version of the facts, side by side with the actual facts as we all recall them. The two versions deal with the same series of crimes, but they identify entirely different people as the wrongdoers who committed them.

The prosecution accuses Panici, Gliottoni and Marshall, the former mayor of Chicago Heights and two former city commissioners. We defendants indignantly deny

198

those charges. What's more, we point the finger of guilt at the prosecution's key witnesses, the very people who have testified against us; LoBue, Prisco, Galderio and Costello. And we don't merely accuse them. We point out to you, the reader, that the prosecution witnesses have all been bribed and coerced to say what the prosecutors tell them to say. If they told the truth they would lose everything. But if they lie and say what they're told to say, they walk.

The great civil liberties lawyer Alan M. Dershowitz, revered professor at Harvard Law School (especially by liberals) tells in his book *The Best Defense* how unscrupulous law enforcement agents often seek to "flip" a criminal and turn him into an informer. In such a case legality, mortality and ethics go right out the window.

*"... the police were sucking him in, deeper and deeper, until he had no one to turn to – except them. This is how the government plays in the deadly game of **trial by informer**, especially when, as is often the case, it's **the only game in town**; the only way of breaking an important case."*

There is no physical evidence to support the prosecutors' case. The FBI's forensic auditors did their best to find physical evidence. They failed. They found no telltale trail of unaccounted for money. How was that possible, if the three defendants really did steal all that money? The simple answer is, there is no money trail because there was never any money to find! There is no *prima facie* case, no "smoking gun" of any kind.

The entire prosecution case rests on the testimony of a known pathological liar, Nick LoBue. This is a man who confesses to having lied throughout his adult life. He tacitly admits to the court that he's lying, each of the 850 times he answers "I don't recall" when we ask him what he really did. He admits to stealing from his own father, defrauding his cousin, defrauding the taxpayers of Chicago Heights by demanding and receiving kickback payments on garbage contracts, liquor licenses, water meter installations, insurance premiums and the biggest kickback of all, $100,000 extorted from the engineering consortium that build the water pipeline to bring fresh drinking water from Lake Michigan to Chicago Heights. There's plenty of physical evidence to convict LoBue!

All the money trails lead to LoBue and only to LoBue. And there the money disappears into LoBue's pocket.

Nick LoBue has confessed to all of these crimes. He pleads guilty. But just look at this! Nick LoBue will not serve a lifetime of consecutive sentences for his lies, extortion rackets and outright theft. No! On the contrary he has won leniency from the government and outright immunity from prosecution for nearly all of his wrongdoing. The same holds true for the three prosecution witnesses who supposedly corroborate LoBue's untruthful testimony: Prisco, Galderio and Costello.

They can't even get their various stories to agree. "I don't recall," has become the mantra of these prosecution witness every time we ask them an inconvenient question. LoBue repeated it 850 times! Each has a significantly different version of the facts. And these different versions in turn differ from the versions filed by the prosecutors. And we are asked to accept these uncoordinated lies as "overwhelming evidence?"

Here is the question. How can you rely on anything these people say, even under oath? What incentive does any of them have to tell the truth and admit their stories are poorly written fiction? What that would get them is long years of imprisonment. On the other hand the prosecutors have given them every incentive to lie through their teeth. That way they get off easy. No problem making that decision! And please notice the common thread that runs through their lies. In every case we clearly see, with physical proof, that these guys were all on the take. Of course they "don't recall!" The truth would put them behind bars for good! And in every case we hear the same pathetic attempt to shift the blame and wiggle off the hook. "Sure, I committed these crimes. But I'm just a little guy, just an underling. You don't want me, Mr. Prosecutor. You want Mr. Big!"

Believe these guys? No way! Not unless the prosecutors can come up with some *disinterested* witnesses - people who have *nothing to gain or lose* from the outcome of the trial, people who can't be influenced with money or promises of special favor. Well guess what? There are very few such witnesses. And the few of those who gave evidence said nothing that implicated the defendants!

So where's the "overwhelming evidence" other than these four bribed and coerced liars?

The prosecutors made a big deal out of the testimony of Betty Tocco, estranged wife of Mob boss Albert Tocco. They're selling the idea that Tocco and Mayor Panici were partners in crime, that Commissioner Marshall approached Tocco and asked to be cut in on the water pipeline kickbacks. In fact Betty Tocco is a red herring. She doesn't know anything. She knows her husband is a big player in the Mob and very little else. These mob bosses play it close to the vest. It's one of their rules. When Betty Tocco says, "I overheard this," or "I heard Albert say on the phone," she has no idea who she's talking about. Was "that black bitch" whom Albert Tocco reportedly spoke of actually City Commissioner Louise Marshall, as the prosecution wants us to think, or was it a member of the Chicago Outfit's far flung prostitution racket? I think we can guess which is more likely.

They sure aren't getting anything out of Tocco himself! He refuses to answer any questions at all. And it's because of Tocco's stony silence that the prosecutors are saying, "Tocco won't talk, so we have to rely on the steel trap memory of our pathological liar, Nick LoBue."

What? You mean Mr. "I-don't-recall 850 times?" That's like firemen saying, "We can't find water to fight this roaring blaze, so we're throwing gasoline on it."

But let's get back to the world of common sense and examine the key unproven accusation the prosecutors have made. They allege that our water commissioner, Louise Marshall, a 70 year old woman, a very successful African American businesswoman, got wind of Nick LoBue's kickback scheme on the water pipeline. They say that Louise approached Mayor Panici and asked to be included in the deal.

Gee! How would they know that? How - without telepathic powers - would anyone know of such a thing even if it were true? Obviously this is one of LoBue's juicier lies, and he's a much more accomplished liar than the other three prosecution witnesses. This one is an exception to his 850 memory failures. But wait. How would LoBue know? Hold that doubt in your mind while we look at LoBue's second and even stupider lie.

The prosecutors go further and say that Louise Marshall, having gotten no satisfaction from the mayor, next went to Albert Tocco with the same request. Well first of all, what interest did Tocco and the Mob have in the city water pipeline kickback? I guess we're supposed to believe that Tocco had the power to order the mayor and his subordinates to split the pie as he directed. The fact is that Albert Tocco and the Chicago Outfit had no finger in that pie. Garbage collection? Sure, they controlled Fitzpatrick Brothers, the waste management company that served the city and for that privilege they greased the palm of Nick LoBue. But the Mob had no interest in Water Commissioner Louise Marshall and her pipeline project.

Albert "Caesar" Tocco

Even so, let's follow this absurdity right out to the end with one of those "thought experiments" that Stephen Hawking uses for figuring out how the world works. Suppose Panici and Tocco are partners in crime. Suppose Panici is a Mafia influenced mayor, as the feds are trying to make us think.

If that's the case, and LoBue is the mayor's "bag man" - a mere underling - then how come LoBue is here in court testifying as the prosecution's star witness? Why hasn't LoBue met with the sudden unlucky accident that happens to Mob members who betray the Outfit? Why has he not been found upside down in one of his dumpsters? If these city officials were really "connected"

206

do you think LoBue, Galderio, Prisco and Costello would ever have testified in court? And not only the witnesses. How about the jury? You've watched *The Sopranos*. You know how the Mob finds a way to intimidate one juror - just one is all they need - by threatening that juror's wife, children, friends, relatives - whatever it takes.

The couple was driving on a road outside Joliet when they were killed by a shotgun blast on July 2, 1980. Dauber, a hit man, was facing federal drug charges, and Outfit bosses thought he would testify against them, investigators said. The Daubers had just left the courthouse in Joliet and were driving to their home in Crete when they were killed. In 1990, Albert Tocco, reputed south suburban mob boss, was sentenced to 200 years in prison for running his crime family through murder and extortion. Witnesses, including Tocco's wife, implicated him in ordering the killings of the Daubers.

With those gruesome images in mind, what do we make of the prosecutors' story about Louise Marshall "putting the arm" on Albert Tocco and the Mob? Stephen

Hawking and the super-scientists would be polite and give it "low probability." I call it B*ll Sh*t. The lie isn't even clever. It's stupid.

And yet here's FBI "Special" Agent O'Malley telling prosecutor Chris Gair under oath that he interviewed Louise Marshall and that she "confessed" to having asked the Mob for a share of the take because she had heard "the Mafia was fair." Wow! That's quite a confession. I guess the FBI, being the thorough, professional crime fighters that they are, must have had Louise sign a written copy of that confession. Right? And I guess Special Agent O'Malley has a copy of that written and signed confession with him, ready to enter as Exhibit X. Right?

Well ... ahem! ... Special Agent O'Malley actually doesn't have a signed confession to show the court. He doesn't even have an un-signed confession. He doesn't have anything at all in writing to support his story. Not even handwritten notes in his special agent's notebook. I guess Special Agent O'Malley forgot to take his special agent's ballpoint pen with him when he conducted that interview. There is no record whatsoever – none at all -

that any such interview ever took place!

Oh, but guess what! It just so happens that prosecutor Chris Gair was also present when Special Agent O'Malley interviewed Louise Marshall and that he too heard her "confession" about the meeting with Mob boss Tocco. Neither one of them wrote down a single word about the "confession" - so crucial to their case. No surprise that when Louise Marshall herself testifies in her own defense and says, "Mr. Gair, I never told you that" prosecutor Gair goes into his tailspin.

"How can this woman accuse a dedicated FBI special agent of lying under oath?" he splutters. "I was there myself," he tells the (noticeably sympathetic) judge, "I heard it with my own ears."

I'm paraphrasing, but this is the true gist of what was said.

"Well then," Louise's lawyer says, "you'd better swear to that under oath, so that if you're making this up you can be charged with perjury."

"Oh, I don't have to do that," Gair protests. "I don't have to be sworn in as a witness. It's enough that my recollection is the same as Special Agent O'Malley's."

"Maybe. But the Advocate Witness Rule says if a prosecutor wants to enter his own testimony, and wants the court to believe it, he has to get up on the stand and swear to tell the truth, the whole truth and nothing but the truth."

At this point I can mentally hear Chris Gair shrieking, "Objection!" and Judge Zagel instantly snapping "Sustained!" as he usually did. But you know what, gentlemen? You can button your lip and get lost. This is my book, not yours.

Faced with having to repeat his story under oath, Gair pleads with Judge Zagel to let him off the hook. "Just tell the jury not to remember what they just heard me say," he helpfully suggests. And Judge Zagel, always open to helpful suggestions from the prosecution, demonstrates once again what a reasonable judge he is.

"Well, OK," Judge Zagel says, "You don't have to

actually swear under oath that Special Agent O'Malley is telling the truth about this mysterious confession that nobody bothered to write down. I'll instruct the jury to forget that you don't want to swear an oath to tell the truth and just take what you say on the strength of your good character. What we'll say is that you don't have to be sworn as a witness because the defense didn't call you as a witness back at the beginning."

Oh well, that's all right then! Judge Zagel is allowing as evidence a story that's quite plainly a lie. Well, let's be polite and call it "a story lacking any corroboration except the unsworn support of the prosecutor." When Chris Gair refuses to confirm his story under oath he is essentially pointing to himself and whispering with a wink, "I'm lying, folks!" And this learned judge is allowing the story to be heard as <u>evidence</u> even though it will send an innocent woman to prison? Rulings like this make Judge Zagel one of the forgettable names in American justice.

This is one of the truly idiotic features of courtroom procedure – the judge's so-called "injunction" to the jury to disregard what they've just heard. If the consequences weren't so serious it would be hilarious. In fact it does become great comedy when we see the very same logic in the HBO series "Veep," where Julia Louis Dreyfus plays Selena Meyer, fictional female Vice-President of the United States. When she realizes that she has (yet again) made an unfortunate statement to the media, Vice-President Meyer turns on her press assistant and cries, "I need you to make me not to have said that!"

Okay, enough of the prosecution's misdirection, deception and plain lying! Let's go back and see what really happened. Nick Lobue lied, cheated and stole for all of his adult life. He admits that. One of the reasons he stole was to finance a costly gambling habit. Both he and Donald Prisco, former mayor of South Chicago Heights, were habitual gamblers. They were seriously in debt due to their gambling. He began stealing from the taxpayers of Chicago Heights well before he became a city commissioner. He overbilled the city for the water processing material Tri-Lux and pocketed the extra margin. After his election to office he passed the Tri-Lux contract to another supplier but continued to skim a profit off the top.

Collaborating with Ralph Galderio, LoBue extorted money from people seeking favors from the city government. In one case they made a club owner pay them $4000 claiming that they had the ability to arrange for him a license to stay open later at night. The bar operator did eventually get the license but not because of anything LoBue and Galderio did for him. LoBue and Donald Prisco, his gambling associate and partner in a currency exchange business, used the exchange to launder the kickback payments they received from the city garbage contractor, who happened to be Mob boss Albert Tocco, and from other city contractors. Their biggest "score" was when they extorted a $100,000 payment from the engineering group that built the city's new pipeline from Lake Michigan.

In the 1980s Mayor Panici and the commissioners got wind of the corruption that was going on. They asked the FBI to investigate. The investigation did turn up a criminal conspiracy and the FBI diligently traced the money trail to Nick LoBue, Donald Prisco and Ralph Galderio. LoBue's cousin, Rodney Costello was implicated as well. The connection between LoBue and Albert Tocco also came to light. It was an open-and-shut

RICO case with plenty of physical evidence to convict the conspirators.

But then the game changed, and it's easy to see how and why. The feds were looking for bigger game in their anti-corruption campaign. They had LoBue, Prisco, Galderio and Costello dead to rights but that was no great distinction. Just four more small time crooked municipal politicians. Nothing that would make them big headlines.

The guy the feds had their sights on was me, Chuck Panici, a major player in Republican Party politics, Republican committeeman for Bloom Township, acquaintance of presidents Reagan and Bush, friend of senators, governors and congressmen. When Republican governor "Big Jim" Thompson recommended James B. Zagel to President Ronald Reagan for appointment as a judge, Chuck Panici's signature was one of those that approved Zagel's appointment.

There were people in both parties who thought Chuck Panici had gotten too big for his britches. That was surely on the minds of certain people in the Justice

Department when the FBI began watching Panici and looking into his affairs in the mid 1980s, tailing him, tapping his phone calls and tracing his financial dealings. Hundreds of thousands of dollars were spent on a series of investigations that yielded no evidence of wrongdoing. There was nothing to suggest Panici was anything but what he looked like, an honest and successful businessman.

But then LoBue agreed to give them what they wanted if they gave him what he wanted. LoBue wanted leniency, mere token prison time in return for his "cooperation." With the support of the other three conspirators he offered to denounce the mayor and two of the city's other three commissioners. In return LoBue, Prisco, Galderio and Costello would get light sentences. Some would get complete immunity. There remained the lack of physical evidence, but the feds had ways of snookering an indictment past a grand jury without necessarily producing real evidence. Remember the Santiago Proffer? They know how to make appearance pass for reality. That was what set in motion the elaborate web of lies, half-truths deception and misdirection that we have seen throughout this entire legal proceeding. The smoke-

and-mirrors prosecution was successful, thanks to the constant cooperation of Judge Zagel and the usual cheerleading of the media. Who can say whether the prosecutors threatened Zagel with "Obstruction of Justice" - their favorite catch-all charge - if he failed to support their case? We've seen that's a common form of prosecutor misconduct, and they certainly did enjoy his support from start to finish. Or maybe his history as a lawyer who worked exclusively as a prosecutor just makes him see the world through prosecutor colored glasses.

Since 1970 there have been 2500 cases like ours in the United States, cases where prosecutors, and sometimes judges, have sent innocent people to prison by abusing their discretion and powers. That's why we now have the Innocence Project, founded in 1992 by two New York law professors and now active throughout the United States and abroad, challenging unfair verdicts primarily in death penalty cases but also dealing with unjust non-capital convictions.

But back to the question. Did they prove their case beyond reasonable doubt? Do   you believe Nick

LoBue, "Mr. I-Don't-Recall 850 times?" Equally important – do you honestly believe that hard working, successful business people like Louise Marshall, John Gliottoni and myself would risk disgrace and imprisonment for the sake of $625 a month in illicit income? That's what the total "take" alleged in the prosecutors' indictment actually works out to.

They alleged that in total we had taken in "over $600,00 in bribes and kickbacks." That's the most impressive number they could come up with. And it has no basis in fact. Where did they get a number like that? From Nick LoBue of course. And we have seen how reliable an informant Nick LoBue is ... NOT!

But let's be credulous simpletons and work with that imaginary number. Supposedly there were five participants in the alleged conspiracy. The first, and without question the greediest, was Nick LoBue. Then came Donald Prisco, Chuck Panici, John Gliottoni and Louise Marshall. On average that's a five-way split on the take. $600,000 divided by five is $120,000 apiece over the 16 years of this supposedly "so corrupt" administration. That's $7,500 apiece per year, which in turn divides up into an average monthly share of $625. I was reporting about $18,750 of monthly income, so that $625 would have upped the figure by 3.3%.

Well, jinkies! Is that enough to make us risk our necks? I don't believe it and I'm sure you don't either. Remember, the sums that the prosecution trumpeted throughout the trial came out of thin air. Supposedly they're products of LoBue's "curiously selective" memory. They're not among the 850 things he is unable to recall. I made a different calculation earlier in this book which is no more alluring to a prospective conspirator than this one is. Come on, folks! It just doesn't make sense.

Rita Crundwell, the embezzling treasurer of Dixon, Illinois, worked with better odds. She was risking her neck for $2.5 million a year. But she still got caught. These people always get caught sooner or later. I can see that very clearly. I'm sure you can too. I'm sure Judge Zagel saw it, although it shouldn't surprise us that he didn't point it out to the jury. The jury quite obviously didn't notice the prosecutors' ridiculous arithmetic. They didn't notice because, like skillful stage magicians, the prosecutors directed the jury's attention elsewhere.

With you it's different. Yours is the opinion that matters. You have seen the facts in the clear light of day. The prosecutors have not been able to work their smoke-and-mirror tricks with you.
With the truthful evidence that you have been shown, and having seen through the prosecutors' sleight of hand, I ask you to enter on behalf of Charles Panici, John Gliottoni and Louise Marshall the verdict that should have been given in 1993, "Not guilty."

Glossary of Names and Terms

A. A. Arken – The pest control company through which Nick LoBue billed Albert Tocco's waste disposal company, Chicago Heights Disposal, for pest control services that were never rendered. The payments were in fact kickback commissions for awarding Tocco the city contract.

Advocate Witness Rule -- The principle that prohibits an attorney from serving as an advocate and a witness in the same case. Also known as the *Lawyer-Witness Rule*, it
was violated in an unusual way during Louise Marshall's trial by prosecutor Chris Gair. Gair offered his own unsworn testimony when the veracity of an undocumented confession was challenged by the supposed confessee. Judge James B. Zagel admitted Gair's unsworn testimony and on appeal the circuit court, on an obscure technicality, upheld his ruling.

Alan M. Dershowitz – "America's most peripatetic civil liberties lawyer." Brooklyn born lawyer, jurist and political commentator. Became a full professor at the Harvard Law School at the age of 28. As a criminal appellate lawyer has won 87% of his cases. Overturned the conviction of Claus von Bulow in 1984 and advised the defense in the O.J. Simpson trial of 1995. In his popular book, *The Best Defense*, Dershowitz tells of a case that makes us think of Nick LoBue, *"... the police were sucking him in, deeper and deeper, until he had no one to turn to – except them. This is how the government plays in the deadly game of trial by informer."*

Al Pilotto – An important *caporegime* of the Chicago Outfit notorious for plundering the assets of the Laborers' International Union

Albert Caesar Tocco – A senior boss of the Chicago Outfit who operated principally in the southern suburb of Chicago Heights. In the Panici-Gliottoni-Marshall trial prosecutors sought to portray Tocco as the criminal master mind of a conspiracy that reached into the Chicago Heights city government. No physical evidence of such a conspiracy was ever produced, nor any credible testimony other than the four convicted felons who testified – untruthfully - against the defendants.

Allan A. Ackerman, PC – One of Chicago's most capable and colorful defense attorneys. Famous for his Gene Autry style western dress, Ackerman practices almost exclusively in the area of criminal defense, both at the trial and appellate levels. His work is the subject of study in law schools throughout the nation. Ackerman argued Chuck Panici's unsuccessful appeals but was not engaged by Panici until the end of the actual trial.

Andrew P. Napolitano -- A former New Jersey Superior Court judge, now political and senior judicial analyst for Fox News Channel. In books like *The Constitution In Exile*, Judge Napolitano is scathingly critical of federal prosecutors for violating their own laws in order to get convictions.

Anthony Onesto – John Gliottoni's principal defense counsel. Famous for asking, "Why do so many people assume that anybody whose name ends in a vowel is involved in organized crime?

Audio Recording – The practice of making sound recordings of police interviews and witnesses' statements in order to ensure completeness and accuracy, familiar to all who watch British crime drama *(Prime Suspect, DCI Banks)* but, oddly, not used by the FBI. *(See Form FD-302)*

Bagman – A courier who collects money on behalf of senior public figures so that funds are delivered in a secret or confidential manner.

Bench Trial – A trial in which a judge, sitting alone without a jury, hears evidence and decides the verdict. Though rare in the United States it is an option open to defendants in other Common Law countries. Many jurists believe the Bench Trial produces a fairer hearing and better informed verdict than a *Jury Trial*.

Bob Picha – A leading facilitator of the *Adventures In Attitudes* program and a longtime friend of Chuck Panici. Now a widely sought-after speaker and workshop leader.

Brady Rule –The US Supreme Court has ruled that prosecutors must disclose evidence or information favorable to the defendant in a criminal case even if not specifically requested. Judge Zagel failed to enforce this rule in the Panici trial.

Brief -- A written legal argument stating the legal reasons for an action, citing statutes, regulations, case precedents, legal texts, and reasoning applied to the particular facts of the case. A brief sets forth the argument for various petitions and motions before the court.

Cesare Panici – Father of Chuck Panici. Immigrated in the early 1900s from the Italian region of Lazio, south of Rome, to settle in Chicago Heights, Illinois, where he married Josephine Cimaroli, a girl from his home town of Amaseno, Frosinone, Italy.

Charles "Chuck" Panici – Middle son of Cesare and Josephine Panici, four-term mayor of Chicago Heights and influential Republican Party functionary. Imprisoned for eight years on corruption charges relating to bribes and kickbacks which were later held to be the work of the prosecution's main witness, finance commissioner Nick LoBue. Continues to advise political candidates and to lead attitudinal self-improvement training.

Charles Fitzpatrick – Founding co-owner of the Fitzpatrick Brothers waste disposal company, the business later acquired by Albert Tocco.

Charles Swindoll -- Evangelical Christian pastor, author, educator, and radio preacher. Founder of the syndicated radio program *Insight for Living* and author of more than 70 books.

Chicago Heights – A southern suburb of Metropolitan Chicago in Cook County, Illinois, nicknamed "Crossroads of the Nation" for its concentrated industrial development.

Chris Gair -- A trial attorney who now specializes in white-collar criminal defense, antitrust and high-stakes commercial litigation, most of them jury trials in the federal courts. Gair was an assistant US attorney in 1993 and led the prosecution of Panici, Gliottoni and Marshall. Like many Justice Department lawyers, Gair is said to have engaged in *Prosecutorial Misconduct*, for which existing US law provides no remedy.

Common Law – The body of legal principles established by practice and custom rather than legislation. Originating in England, the common law now prevails in all English speaking countries, including the states of the US and the federal government.

Dante Alighieri – Major Italian poet of the Middles Ages and author of *The Divine Comedy*, whose best known book is *The Inferno*. Considered the Father of the Italian language because his Florentine dialect later evolved into modern Italian..

Dante DeSantis – Professional engineer, WW2 veteran, former mayor of Glenwood, IL and senior partner in Robinson Engineering, DeSantis was a victim of Nick LoBue's water pipeline kickback scheme, coerced into funneling $100,000 to LoBue. His testimony identified LoBue as the extortionist but did not implicate Panici, Gliottoni or Marshall.

Dolores (Falcioni) Panici – For 42 years beloved wife of Charles "Chuck" Panici and mother of Debbie, Charles Jr., Joseph and Tami Panici.

Dominic "Mimi" Falaschetti – Schoolmate of Chuck Panici, Sam "Hobo" Cianchetti, Giulio "Mccollough" Perozzi et al. First of the group to go to college. Became an art teacher.

Donald Prisco – Former mayor of neighboring South Chicago Heights, business and gambling associate of Nick LoBue, co-owner of the currency exchange that laundered bribes and kickbacks. Testified for the prosecution in return for leniency.

Ed Derwinski – Congressman representing south and southwest suburbs of Chicago and later Secretary of Veterans Affairs under President George H. W. Bush.

Eugene Sadus – A former Bloom High School teacher who served as a Chicago Heights elected official from 1975 till 1991. Sadus was Sanitation Commissioner during the LoBue-Tocco garbage contract bribery era but was not indicted or called as a witness.

Fitzpatrick Brothers – The waste disposal company that until 1983 collected garbage in Chicago Heights. Albert Tocco bought the company in 1983 and renamed it Chicago Heights Disposal.

Form FD-302 – A form used by FBI agents to report or summarize the interviews that they conduct, containing information from notes taken during a verbal interview. This method differs little from those of the 18th century, whereas the police of most other nations have long relied on audio recording technology for its accuracy and security. Nothing guarantees the truth or authenticity of an FD-302 report except the unsworn word of an FBI agent. Sadly, FBI agents have not always told the truth.

Fourth Amendment to the Constitution of the United States -- A part of the Bill of Rights which guards against unreasonable searches and seizures and requires any warrant to be judicially sanctioned and supported by probable cause. Its intent and effect was to guarantee due process of law in a criminal proceeding. The RICO statute of 1972 nullifies the protections of the Fourth Amendment in cases where criminal conspiracy is alleged. *(see RICO Statute)*

Francis Fukuyama – American political scientist, economist and author best known for his book *The End of History and the Last Man*. Associated with the rise of American neoconservative movement, from which he later distanced himself. *(see Prosecutorial Misconduct)*

Fred Foreman – US Attorney for Chicago at the time of the Panici-Gliottoni-Marshall trial, later made a judge of the Federal Court.

Fred LoBue – A senior Republican Party functionary at the time when Chuck Panici was entering politics. LoBue supported Panici's campaign financially and rhetorically. A namesake but not a relative of Nick LoBue.

Fritz Nehnevay – Chuck Panici's co-chair in the referendum campaign of 1963 that raised $10 million for school funding in Chicago Heights.

George M. O'Brien – Republican congressman representing 17ᵗʰ Illinois Congressional District from 1973 till 1986. A colleague, friend and supporter of Chuck Panici.

George Robert Blakey – Attorney and law professor who, working with Senator John L. McClellan, drafted the *Racketeering Influenced and Corrupt Organizations Act* (RICO). The RICO statute, though highly effective, is criticized for going too far with its open-ended language and vague definitions but has not been repealed or amended.

George Santayana – Philosopher, essayist, poet and novelist famous for the maxim, "Those who cannot remember the past are condemned to repeat it."

Grand Jury -- A panel of citizens, usually of 23 to 25 members, convened to decide whether it is appropriate for the government to indict (proceed with a prosecution against) someone suspected of a crime. Most common law countries and half of the states of the Union have abandoned the grand jury, replacing it with the judicial *preliminary hearing* which, unlike the grand jury, hears evidence from both prosecution and defense, is subject to the Rules of Evidence and is decided by a judge rather than a group of lay people.

Hearsay Evidence – The unverified report by a witness of someone else's words, usually disallowed as evidence in a court of law. Apart from the mutual corroboration of the government's four bribed and coerced witnesses, the case against Panici, Gliottoni and Marshall relied wholly on hearsay evidence.

Humpty Dumpty – The oversize animated egg of the nursery rhyme, one of the best known in the English-speaking world. In Lewis Carroll's *Through The Looking Glass* Humpty Dumpty explains to Alice his peculiar way of making words mean exactly what he wants them to mean, very much like lawyers' and judges' legal jargon.

Hungry Hill (The Hill) – The southeast corner of Chicago Heights, first populated heavily by Italian and Central European immigrants. Some locals say "Hungry" is a corruption of "Hungary" but no one believes it refers literally to hunger. The term "Hill" is a bigger mystery because there is no upward slope of the land anywhere on "The Hill."

Improper Argument – A term covering several types of lawyers' misdemeanor that can be the basis for overturning a trial verdict on appeal. One of the meanings of "Improper Argument" is "injecting facts not in evidence," as Chris Gair and Marsha McClellan so blatantly did in the Panici-Gliottoni-Marshall trial. While attorneys are given a lot of room to argue reasonable inferences from the evidence, they may not argue a fact that is not supported by the evidence. Gair and McClellan spoke repeatedly to the jury of allegations that had nowhere been supported by evidence. It was argued that Judge Zagel erred when he failed to distinguish "uncorroborated allegation" from "evidence." The circuit court, typically, opted to uphold the trial judge and jury.

James "Big Jim" Thompson – Republican governor of Illinois for four consecutive terms over a period of 14 years. He announced his candidacy in 1976 at the Panici family's 3 Star lounge in Chicago Heights, due largely to Chuck Panici's powerful political support.

James B. Zagel -- The United States District Court judge for Northern Illinois who conducted the Panici-Gliottoni-Marshall trial. Zagel never practiced as a defense attorney. He began his career as a prosecutor and was still a prosecutor when President Ronald Reagan made him a federal judge in 1987, although from 1980 till 1987 he had been Director of the Illinois State Police. Because of his exclusively prosecutorial background, Zagel has been called a "hanging judge." Ironically, one of the political functionaries who approved Zagel's recommendation would have been Bloom Township Republican committeeman Chuck Panici!

James Burke – Mayor of Dixon, Illinois during the

Rita Crundwell Scandal (q.v.)

Jerry Colangelo – Boyhood neighbor of Chuck Panici who became a prominent basketball coach, team owner, sports executive and, most recently, manager of USA Basketball, selecting and managing American teams for international competition.

Joe Panici – Chuck Panici's elder brother, died during World War 2.

John Connally – 39th governor of Texas, Secretary of the Navy under John F. Kennedy and Secretary of the Treasury under Richard M. Nixon. Ran unsuccessfully against Ronald Reagan for the Republican presidential nomination.

John Gliottoni – Commissioner in the Chuck Panici administration of Chicago Heights. A successful and prosperous construction contractor, "Johnny G" was accused of receiving bribes equivalent to an absurdly small fraction of his lawful income.

Judicial Misconduct – Improper actions or behaviour on the part of judges, the counterpart of Prosecutorial Misconduct. Wikipedia's definition states in part, "Actions that can be classified as judicial misconduct include: conduct prejudicial to the effective and expeditious administration of the business of the courts; using the judge's office to obtain special treatment for friends or relatives;

accepting bribes, gifts, or other personal favors related to the judicial office; having improper discussions with parties or counsel for one side in a case; treating litigants or attorneys in a demonstrably egregious and hostile manner; violating other specific, mandatory standards of judicial conduct, such as those pertaining to restrictions on outside income and requirements for financial disclosure; and conduct occurring outside the performance of official duties if the conduct might have a prejudicial effect on the administration of the business of the courts among reasonable people." *(see Prosecutorial Misconduct)*

Kelo Panici – Chuck Panici's brother.

Louise Marshall – Former Chicago Heights water commissioner and co-defendant in the Panici-Gliottoni-Marshall trial. At her sentencing Ms. Marshall both scolded and forgave the prosecutors for railroading her to prison and Judge Zagel for allowing them to, saying, *"Your honor, I would like to say that I would pray for you, Mr. Gair, and your children and your wife. I will pray for Mr. O'Malley (an FBI agent involved in her case). I don't have any hate. I have no envy. You know yourself that I was treated wrong. You know that everything was turned around that was handled. But I wish you well and I hope that your children grow up to be the finest people in the world."*

Marsha McClellan – An assistant US attorney who took part in the Panici-Gliottoni-Marshall trial. Like

232

Chris Gair, McClellan is alleged to have engaged in Prosecutorial Misconduct. Her final argument in the Louise Marshall case is clearly improper in that it assumes facts that were never established in evidence. The rules for prosecutors are clear … *The prosecutor is the servant of the law whose interest in a prosecution is not merely to emerge victorious, but to see that justice is done. He (or she) must avoid insinuations and assertions calculated to mislead the jury.*

Marty Wondaal – Co-owner of Fitzpatrick Brothers waste disposal company.

Miriam Santos – Former Chicago City Treasurer appointed in 1989 by Mayor Richard Daley and Democrat candidate in 1999 for Illinois attorney general, convicted in 1999 of mail fraud and attempted extortion. Her defense attorney was none other than Chris Gair, who had prosecuted the Panici trial six years earlier, and who famously told the court, "[A witness] who has been granted immunity … cannot be trusted." *(sic!)* Ms. Santos's conviction was overturned on appeal in 2000 because Judge Richard Posner of the Circuit Court found "a veritable avalanche of errors" committed by trial judge Charles Norgle Sr. Late in 2000 she pleaded guilty to one count of mail fraud and was released.

Motion In Limine – A pre-trial motion "on the threshold" to modify pleadings or establish in advance the particular ground rules of a trial.

Motion to Recuse – Either before or during a trial, counsel for either side may move to *recuse* (replace) a judge for unfair bias. The motion must allege bias beyond judicial rulings against the complaining party. It must also be extra-judicial bias such as improper communication with counsel for either side or a demonstrated racial, ethnic or religious prejudice. In the case of Judge Zagel, the probability that Panici as a Republican committeeman had given written assent to Zagel's judicial appointment was sufficient for a Motion to Recuse.

Napoleon Hill – Author of *Think And Grow Rich* and founder of the self-motivating attitudinal school. Together with W. Clement Stone and others, a long time mentor of Chuck Panici.

Neal O'Malley – FBI agent, now retired, who testified that Louise Marshall had "confessed" to him her involvement in a bribery extortion scheme. O'Malley was able to produce no corroborating evidence of any meeting with Marshall, much less a confession. He possessed no audio recording of the purported confession, nor a signed statement, nor even an un-signed statement, nor even handwritten notes indicating a time and place. Despite the pathetic deficiencies of O'Malley's story, Judge

234

Zagel admitted it and the "brilliant" *(see Posner)* Judge Richard Posner upheld the ruling on appeal.

Nick LoBue – A member of the Chicago Heights City council from 1979 till 1991, accused of abusing his position for the purpose of obtaining bribes and kickback payments. After being indicted and convicted on RICO charges together with his business and gambling associate Donald Prisco, LoBue began to "remember" additional details of his bribery and kickbacks scheme, which included other city officials, notably Mayor Chuck Panici and commissioners John Gliottoni and Louise Marshall. These new "memories" coincided with a plea bargaining deal that dropped the RICO charges against LoBue in return for his testimony against Panici, Gliottoni and Marshall. LoBue signed an agreement with federal prosecutors in 1991, pleading guilty to filing a false tax return and conspiring to commit extortion. Chicago Heights filed civil lawsuits in 1992 resulting in $7.8 million in judgments against LoBue and 20 other defendants. He moved to Albuquerque, New Mexico in 1992.

Phil Panici – Elder brother of chuck Panici. Died in March 1992 just before Chuck Panici was indicted and about a week after the death of Chuck's wife Dolores.

Preliminary Hearing -- A proceeding used in most common law countries, after a criminal complaint has been filed by the prosecutor, to determine whether there is enough evidence to require a trial. In the United States, the judge must find <u>probable cause</u> that a crime was committed if an indictment is to proceed. Unlike a Grand Jury proceeding a preliminary hearing allows the accused to have legal counsel, cross examine witnesses and inspect documents. *(see Grand Jury)*

Prima Facie -- Latin for "at first look," or "on the face of it," referring to a lawsuit or criminal prosecution in which pre-trial evidence appears sufficient to prove the case unless the defense produces evidence to the contrary. In a Grand Jury proceeding a number of checks written on a non-existent bank account would make a prima facie case and would result in an indictment. But in a Preliminary Hearing, proof that the bank had misprinted the account number on the checks might kill the case and halt the proceeding.

Prosecutorial Misconduct – The "win-at-any-cost" tactics that include, for example, withholding evidence, misleading jurors and suborning perjury. All of the foregoing are alleged against Chris Gair and Marsha McClellan in the Panici-Gliottoni-Marshall trial. Appeal courts rarely recognize these tactics as wrongdoing. Usually they rely on the doctrine of "harmless error" contending (often unfairly) that the misconduct did not infringe the right of the accused to a fair trial.

Ralph Galderio – A longtime friend of Chuck Panici but not the bosom buddy portrayed by the prosecution and the media. Galderio and Panici knew each other from their school days and Panici was best man at Galderio's wedding. But Galderio was a perennial opportunist ever on the lookout for the "easy touch." Panici got him a job with the City of Chicago Heights and employed Thelma Galderio as his secretary. But when caught extorting kickbacks along with Nick LoBue, Galderio made a plea bargain and turned on Panici by purporting to corroborate LoBue's untruthful testimony. Galderio's account often differed from that of LoBue, which in turn differed from what the prosecutors had filed in court.

Richard Posner – Respected judge of the US Court of Appeals for the 7th Circuit and senior judge of the three who heard the Panici-Gliottoni-Marshall appeal. One of President Reagan's "activist" appointees, Posner is considered a "pragmatist" rather than an "ideologue." Criticized by many lawyers for his willingness to "write law" (set new precedents in case law) instead of confining himself to "reading the law." Posner's written judgment on the Panici appeal is less perceptive than one would expect of a jurist some say is "too brilliant" for a seat on the Supreme Court of the United States. He would not get along with a "reader of the law" like SCOTUS Justice Antonin Scalia.

RICO Statute – They say the camel is "a horse designed by a committee." The RICO statute of 1972 was a similar collaborative project, led by Robert George Blakey and Senator John L. McClellan. The much needed goal of the *Racketeer Influenced and Corrupt Organizations Act* was to flush out and prosecute the criminal organizations that so often hid behind the façade of legal enterprises like the Teamsters' Union. But like many committees the lawmakers fell short in some respects while going too far in others. Lawyers and jurists deplore the vague and often open-ended language that makes RICO a tool for prosecuting lawful businesses as well as criminal enterprises. One of RICO's deficiencies is that it ignores the *due process* guarantees of the Fourth Amendment.

Rita Crundwell – Former comptroller of the town of Dixon, Illinois, boyhood home of President Ronald Reagan. Charged with and convicted in 2012 of embezzling $53 million in city funds over a 20-year period.

Rodney Costello – A cousin of Nick LoBue and an occasional co-conspirator in arranging bribes and kickbacks. Costello was one of the four felons who were granted immunity or leniency in exchange for their lies on the witness stand.

Rules of Evidence – The code of Evidence Law governing whether, how, and for what purpose evidence may be offered to a judge or jury in support of a case. Judge Zagel's admission of the unsworn testimony of prosecutor Chris Gair against Louise Marshall violated the Advocate Witness Rule, which is one of the Rules of Evidence, but was allowed to stand by the appeal judges with the outrageous excuse that it "did not prejudice the defendant's right to a fair trial."

Sam "Hobo" Cianchetti – Boyhood neighbor and lifelong friend of Chuck Panici, later a judge of the Superior Court of California.

Santiago Proffer – Named for the drug trafficking case in which it was first used, a proffer of evidence that outlines the case prosecutors intend to allege against an accused.

Sir Walter Scott – British novelist, poet and scholar whose family estate at Abbotsford, Scotland has become a shrine to romantic literature. Author of the couplet, *"Oh, what a tangled web we weave: When first we practice to deceive!"*

Sixth Amendment -- The part of the United States Bill of Rights that stipulates the rights of a person charged with a crime. The Supreme Court has applied the provisions of this amendment to the states through the Due Process Clause of the Fourteenth Amendment.

Spilotro Brothers – Anthony and Michael Spilotro were Chicago Outfit members who rose to prominence in Las Vegas during the era of Mob owned casinos in the 1970s. Both were executed in 1986 in a hunting lodge owned by Tony Spilotro's former boss, Joey Aiuppa and buried in an Indiana cornfield. Among the prime suspects was Albert Tocco, but his involvement was never proven.

Subornation of Perjury – The act of inducing or allowing a witness to lie under oath, as the prosecutors so obviously did with their four plea bargaining witnesses, LoBue, Prisco, Galderio and Costello.

Thelma Galderio – Wife of Ralph Galderio *(q.v.)* and secretary to Mayor Chuck Panici during his administration. Divorced Ralph Galderio following the plea bargain with the feds that led to his testifying against Panici.

Tri-Lux – The water treatment chemical used for many years to reduce the mineral content of the Chicago Heights well water. The contract to supply it was one of Nick LoBue's overbill-kickback schemes.

US vs. Boyd – A weapons offense case heard in the Court of Appeal for the 7th Circuit in 2007. The original trial was in Indiana state court where Artemus Boyd was charged with firing six shots into the air while leaving a nightclub at 3 am. Judge Richard Posner wrote a verdict that has been severely criticized by law professor Douglas Berman for grossly overstepping the federal court's jurisdiction. Berman writes, *"On appeal, no one (including the Seventh Circuit judges) seem to question whether it was sensible for a federal district judge to try and sentence a federal defendant for a disputed state offense. Instead, Judge Posner essentially conducts his own philosopher-king bench trial."*

W. Clement Stone – Famous American businessman and one of Chuck Panici's inspirational mentors. Famous Stone aphorisms include, *"Whatever the mind of man can conceive and believe, it can achieve."* A maxim that sustained Chuck Panici through all his adversities is **Og Mandino's Persistence Motto**, *"I will persist until I succeed. The prizes of life are at the end of each journey, not near the beginning; and it is not given to me to know how many steps are necessary* *to reach my goal. One step at a time is not too difficult."*

William A. Fischel – Academic, educator and author. Professor of economics and legal affairs at Dartmouth College, New Hampshire. A vocal critic of the RICO statute who warns of the need to restrain over zealous prosecutors who could easily use RICO in ways that Congress never intended. This has in fact already happened. The open-ended language of the statute has been used to prosecute not only criminal conspiracies but also law abiding corporations denounced by their competitors.

APPENDIX
Napoleon Hill's Rules of Accurate Thinking

In this book I've said less than I would have liked to say about Napoleon Hill.

This amazing American thinker was born in a one-room cabin in Pound, Virginia in the year 1883. Hill was a classic self-made man in the best Horatio Alger tradition. Despite a grindingly poor childhood, he grew up to be a journalist. As a journalist he got the chance in 1908 to interview Andrew Carnegie, one of the richest and most powerful men in the world at that time. From Carnegie, Hill learned that the process of personal success could be outlined in a simple formula that anyone could understand and achieve if they were so motivated.

With that knowledge Napoleon Hill went on to become a pioneer in the modern American field of *personal-success literature*. In 1937 he wrote his greatest book, *Think And Grow Rich*, which became one of the best sellers of all time. The focus of the book, and of all of Napoleon Hill's writing, is how achievement actually occurs and how Andrew

Carnegie's achievement formula enables the average person to succeed in life.

As I wrote in Chapter 2 of this book, attitudinal training has been central to everything I've accomplished and Napoleon Hill has been one of my most important mentors. Even a catastrophe like the events of this book takes on a special meaning when we see it in terms of Napoleon Hill's *Rules of Accurate Thinking*. It would serve the cause of justice if every jury member were to read and remember these rules.

2 Simple Fundamental Types Of Reasoning: Inductive and Deductive

- Inductive – where you don't have the facts
- Deductive – where you do have the facts and can separate fact from fiction

Important and Unimportant facts

- What is an important fact and how do you distinguish it from an unimportant fact?
- An important fact will aid you in some way in attaining your major purpose in life.

Opinions

Most opinions are without value because they are based on bias, prejudice, intolerance, guesswork, hearsay or ignorance.

"I cannot answer your question because I have no facts on which to base my opinion." Woodrow Wilson.

A simple rule to avoid being misled by other people:
When you hear someone make a statement that your reason cannot accept as sound or that you question, ask a simple question:

"How do you know?"
Force the speaker to reveal the source; or reject the statement as false.

* Never accept the opinions of other people as being facts until you have learned the source of those opinions and satisfied yourself of their accuracy.
* Free advice is worth exactly what it costs.
* Alert yourself immediately if someone talks slanderously as this should indicate that the statement is based on bias.
* Never disclose what you want the information to be.

* Anything that exists in the universe can be proved. Where no such proof is available it's safer to assume none exists.
* Truth and falsehood carry with them a silent and invisible means of determining whether they are true or false.
* Follow the habit of asking, "How do you know?" Study yourself carefully. You may discover that your emotions are your greatest handicap in the business of accurate thinking. It is easy for you to believe that which you wish to believe … and most people do.

Books on Related Topics

The American System of Criminal Justice
Actual Innocence: When Justice Goes Wrong and How to Make it Right
Prosecution Complex: America's Race to Convict and Its Impact on the Innocent

Made in the USA
Lexington, KY
26 July 2013